This Was Not Supposed To Happen

KINGSLEY GRANT

Copyright © 2011 Kingsley Grant

All rights reserved. No part of this book may be reproduced or transmitted in any form by any means: graphic, electronic, or mechanical. This includes photocopying, recording, taping, podcasting, or via any information storage or retrieval, except where allowed by law in the case of quotations and/or for academic use.

Published by Kingsley Grant, in association with CreateSpace

P.O. Box 4723

Hollywood, Fl. 33083

ISBN-13:
978-0615467504 (Kingsley Grant)

ISBN-10:
0615467504

Unless otherwise attributed, all biblical references are used with permission from the New Living Translation (NLT) of the Holy Bible, by Tyndale House Publishing, Wheaton, IL. (1996):

Joan Harrison
1142 N.W. 85th Ave
Plantation
Fl. 33322

CONTENTS

	Acknowledgments	i
	Dedication	iii
1	All I Wanted Was To Go Home	Pg 1
2	This Was Not Supposed To Happen	Pg 7
3	How It All Started	Pg 11
4	Love Requires Words and Actions	Pg 31
5	Be Careful Whom You Go To For Advice	Pg 45
6	Not Everyone Thinks The Same	Pg 65
7	Watch Out For The Bedroom	Pg 79
8	As A Result Of Sexual Trauma	Pg 95
9	When The Dust Settles	Pg 113
10	Put The Lid On Anger!	Pg 137
11	Murder He Wrote	Pg 147
12	For"GIFT"ness	Pg 153
13	Conclusion	Pg 167
	Appendix	Pg 171

ACKNOWLEDGMENTS

This project has been more than twenty years in the making. It has been a long journey but a very rich and rewarding one. It is rich and rewarding because of the many people who have in one way or another, played a pivotal role in my life. I know I will run the risk of overlooking someone who may feel offended that they were not included by name within the covers of this book. If this happens to be you, please forgive me. It was an innocent oversight on my part. The pages of this book would not be adequate to list everyone and say some thing about the role that they played in helping to shape my life.

No one person has been more instrumental in this process than the Person of Jesus Christ through the power of the Holy Spirit. It would have been impossible for me to do this project without his help. I am a firm believer in the words that he spoke in John 15: that says, without him "you can do nothing."

My immediate family (wife – Dionne, son – Anthony, daughter – Natalie) is my major cheerleader. They are the ones who matters the most to me. Their affirmations, encouragements, and sometimes correction of things I say or do both at home and in public settings are, most important. From them I have learned a great deal.

Another person who gave me great insights in the printing process and served as the main editor, is Katrina Moody. Her expertise was invaluable.

Two of my close friends who have also served as encouragers and have helped me with the editing process, are Gilbert Harris and Madeline Hundy. They have been instrumental in this process. I owe them a great deal. Not only was Madeline involved at this level, but also was also very influential in my educational accomplishments. It was because of her relentless encouragement, support, and belief in me, why I decided to pursue my Masters Degree at the time I did.

I am eternally grateful to all who have prayed for me. Your prayers are of the utmost importance. Thanks a million.

DEDICATION

This book is dedicated to all those who have ever experienced sexual trauma in any form. So many people today are living with the stigma related to sexual abuse and may be wondering if there is any hope for them. There are others who are suffering in silence because of not being able to talk about their experience. Others have spoken about their experience but is still being impacted by what happened to them.

One of the goals of this book is to help those who have been victimized, find hope.

I do understand that there are no easy answers to the pain experienced by sexual trauma. However one of the centerpieces of healing or recovery from such, is that of forgiveness. This virtue must be utilized if one is ever going to be "free". This will be outlined in chapter twelve. You could also read one of my blog entries at *http://www.regainhope.com, which* talks about **"Freedom through Forgiveness"**. More is said about it there.

By using the story of Tamar found within the pages of the Holy Bible, I am hoping to convey a message of hope while highlighting the emotional and physiological stress that is commonly associated with trauma

I want to caution you that this story contains some lurid details, but I believe it parallels many of the stories that have been written or talked about through major media outlets.

Unfortunately the possibility exists that as a reader, you may be able to relate to parts of this story. I pray that this is not true of you. However if it is, you need to make sure you reach out for help and do not continue to live with this pain. I have found that there is a lot of people living with severe emotional pain but doing so alone. They are suffering in silence. This I call the "Suffering In Silence" Syndrome or the S.I.S Syndrome.

I use this term to describe someone who has gone through a possible trauma in their life but kept it to him or herself. They might also be experiencing those traumatic events currently, but because of pride, family loyalty, cultural dictates, religious teaching, or a host of other reasons, have chosen to remain quiet while suffering; hence the term "Suffering In Silence."

I hope this is not you. If it is, I pray that as you read further, you will be given the strength and fortitude to put an end to this suffering. God did not intend for you to live this way. You will find suggestions of helpful resources throughout the book.

I pray that this book will be a blessing to you as you read it. If you find it to be so, pass it on or recommend it to someone who you know would also find it helpful.

CHAPTER ONE

All I wanted was to go home

All I wanted to do was to go home. It was late and public transportation had virtually ended for the night. Public transportation is not something that was readily available after certain hours. Most of what would have been available were taxis for which you had to pay a premium price at that hour of the night.

Working at a job that did not pay much, it would have been a huge payout just to get home at that time of night.

I worked as a bank teller. My job entailed the transaction of deposits and withdrawals for customers. As tellers we were one of the first lines of contact most customers had with the bank; we became the "face" of the bank. The customers' satisfaction was a priority. The teller–customer relationship, could easily form the customer impression of the bank. This simply meant that we, in this case I, had to be very friendly to the customers even when I may not have felt like doing so.

I formed a number of relationships through this experience. They were mostly business relationships even though some extended into personal relationships. It was not unusual for customers to try to bribe us in small ways to get us to take their transactions and process it without them having to wait in line. They wanted that VIP treatment.

This seemed like a way for me to build relationship with people that were considered important. I was called by my first name and these VIP customers would make every effort to say hello outside the banking environment. I felt important especially when it was done by some of the wealthier business people.

One of these customers with whom I developed a relationship, worked at one of Jamaica's premier factories that produced bauxite. Bauxite was one of Jamaica's main sources of revenue. Those who worked there, were paid very well, especially if they were in management or had a degree. This particular customer was one of those important employees. Having him talk to me on a first name basis was special … at least I thought so.

This was the person who came to my "rescue" that night.

Feeling stranded and not knowing what to do, the thought occurred to me to see if the "friend" that I had developed a relationship with, was home. If he was, he might offer to take me home. At least, it was worth the try. What did I have to lose?

My thought was he "owed" me one. This is the least he could do in return for the favors I did for him. I was there when he needed me, now I expected him to be there when I needed him. He lived within walking distance from my place of employment. Walking distance for me as well as many Jamaicans, could easily be between two and four miles and some times even more.

He lived approximately one mile from my job.

Having walked to his house and seeing his car in the driveway, created a sense of relief and optimism.

With confidence in my steps, I approached the front door. I knocked and waited. After what seemed like an eternity, someone finally opened the door. To my delight, it was he – my "friend".

He warmly greeted me and invited me in. I told him of my dilemma thinking that he would sympathize with my situation and without hesitation, take me home. That was my hope.

Instead of offering to take me home, he suggested that I spend the night and then leave early the next morning. At that time public transportation would have been more available. People who had to get to work depended on these taxis and buses.

That sounded like a great idea to me. Not only did I have a place to stay, but he also offered me a meal. Wow. How could I turn down such an offer? This was a better alternative to possibly walking home, which would have taken me several hours. On top of that, I got a free meal. You could say my situation made me very vulnerable. Anything but walking home at this point, would have been acceptable.

We stayed up and talked for about an hour or so. We both had to get up early for work the next morning so we decided to prepare for bed. I began to quickly calculate the sleeping arrangements. He lived in a one-bedroom townhouse, so I just assumed that I would be sleeping on the sofa, while he slept in his bed. I was quite okay with that.

However that was not the plan that he had and I would soon find out why.

More of what happened to me will be shared in later chapters.

My story has made me sensitive to that of Tamar's. You will read the full account of her story throughout this book. However, I have to share some very important background information in the following chapters so that you will have a better idea and understanding of my interpretation of the story. Be patient with the process.

CHAPTER TWO

This was not supposed to happen

Have you ever had something happen to you, a member of your family, or a friend that was not supposed to happen? So many people I know, including myself, as well as the featured story of Tamar, have had something happen to them that were *not* supposed to happen.

This can come as a total surprise while at other times, it was clear as to what was going to happen, but unable to do anything about it. I am not sure which is worse. The bottom line is the end result - the impact it had on the people involved.

It is one thing when you experience unfortunate circumstances at the hand of those outside your family or friendship circle, but when it happens within, it is most often devastating. What happened to Tamar and myself, falls within the latter. In Tamar's case it happened among family members, whereas in my case it happened within the friendship circle.

Tamar's story is found in the Old Testament book of 2 Samuel, Chapter 13. The major players in this story are Amnon, Tamar, and Jonadab. The minor players are Absalom and David. David is the father of Amnon, Tamar, and Absalom.

David was one of the most renowned and revered kings mentioned in the Bible. He is the one who wrote most of the Psalms. These Psalms represent different stages or times in his life. You get to know his heart, thoughts, desires, and dreams as you read the Psalms. He was called "a man after God's own heart" (Acts 13:22).

Absalom and Tamar are full brother and sister while Amnon shares only the same father, David, making him the half brother of both Absalom and Tamar. He is the oldest of David's children.

Jonadab is their cousin, the son of one of David's seven brothers. These names are not made up, though they may sound uncommon or a bit confusing. Don't get bogged down trying to pronounce them and miss the main points of the story. It is important that you are able to distinguish these individuals and their relationship to each other.

You can read the story in its entirety in the Appendix section. It is taken from the New Living Bible (NLT).

One of the contributing factors to sexual violation, is the fact that we are living in a sex-crazed society. We are constantly bombarded by sexual images and messages that are coming at us via different forms of media.

Sex is all around us. It is used to sell cars, clothes, music, movies, magazines, hygiene products, and the list goes on and on. There is so much of it around us that it is almost impossible to go through a day without encountering some aspect of it.

Is it any wonder that so many young people are confused on issues pertaining to sex? Is it any wonder so many children are becoming sexually active at an early age?

They hear from some so-called experts that sex is good and that they should not restrain themselves as long as they take precaution, because it is unreasonable to think a young person can restrain their hormonal urges. Still others say that sex outside of marriage is wrong and that they should practice abstinence until marriage.

If this confusion was not enough, add to that the pressure that comes from others who say that if you are not having sex, then something must be wrong with you. They are sometimes even led to believe that they must be dealing with same sex issues.

What should they do with all these messages? Who should they believe?

One of the goals of using Tamar's story, is to point out that human behavior has not really changed over all these years.

Solomon, considered to be the wisest person (other than Jesus), said in Ecclesiastes 1:9, "history merely repeats itself. It has all been done before. Nothing under the sun is truly new." This statement was made a few thousand years ago, but is still true today.

CHAPTER THREE

How it all started

Tamar lived in Israel along with the rest of her family. We do not know if she had any other siblings at this point other than Amnon and Absalom.

Her name means "Palm Tree" – one who is upright, erect, and firm. Names had meanings within her culture as they do in some cultures today. You may have been given your name because of a certain meaning your parents attached to it. It is given as a way of remembrance.

Some parents name their child in remembrance of the conditions surrounding their birth. Others give names, envisioning something about the child or what they would like for that child to become.

My wife and I gave our son and daughter names that had a certain "ring" to it because we are believing that one day they will make a difference in their world. When that happens, people will have an easier time pronouncing and remembering their names. It is said that the grandmother of Jackie Kersey Joyner named the child Jackie, "because someday she is going to be first lady of something!" Jackie, having overcome a birth defect, went on to become the first lady of track and field.

I'm sure David and Tamar's mom had this in mind when they named her as is true of other parents of their time. I wonder if Tamar was doing her best to live up to that name – one who is upright and poised? Children tend to do this.

She was a virgin, a young woman of virtue and incredible character. Character is defined as what you do when no one is looking. She had strong convictions, high moral standards, and self-respect. Sadly, these traits are rare today.

Someone once said, "Beauty is skin deep." This means that some people's beauty doesn't go beyond the top layer of their skin. It's all about what you see. Nothing more. There is not a whole lot more to that person. Below the surface these individuals can be very "ugly" in their attitude. Not only do they lack a "beautiful" attitude, but they are also lacking in the areas of grace and intellect. Their beauty is "lost" once they open their mouth to speak. You wish they had kept their mouth closed.

> *"Beauty is skin deep."*

In today's culture, we see many who have been blessed with physical beauty who try to use it to their advantage. Some use it for personal gain. There are some who think only about themselves. They think they are better than others, especially those who may not have been blessed as they are in the area of physical beauty. Maybe you know some people who fit this description.

Beauty can have its advantages and disadvantages. Beautiful people can sometimes be very lonely. This happens when others are intimidated by them and feel that such a beautiful person would not want to associate with anyone who does not have similar beauty. Sometimes this is farthest from the truth. I recall hearing a story of a very beautiful celebrity whose name I cannot recall. She stated that during her teenage years, she did not have many dates and the few parties she attended, she sometimes ended up having no one to dance with. She later found out from her friends that the general assumptions were that she did not want to dance, would probably say no if asked, or must have already been approached.

I envision Tamar as one who could relate to such a story. Even though there is little said about her beauty, I think for Amnon to be so obsessed with her, she must have been, very attractive.

If I could say anything negative about Tamar it would be that she was a little too trusting as was true in my case as you will see in subsequent chapters. You could say she did not have the "street smarts" to realize the tricks that some guys will employ and the level they will stoop to fulfill their own selfish desire.

Amnon and his desires

Amnon's name means "faithful". However as you will find out in the subsequent chapters, his behavior was far from being truly faithful. It was quite the opposite. He developed an insatiable sexual desire for Tamar. He lusted after her.

Lust is the ultimate act of selfishness. It is selfish because it seeks to satisfy self and self-only. It is not thinking about the interest of the other person. If you feed your lust it will grow into a monster as will be seen by Amnon's actions as the story develops.

As lust grows, it takes more "food" to feed it; it becomes greedy. It begins with "petting" a seemingly innocent act. We "pet" an "innocent" looking magazine or video but then it grows. The best environment for it to grow is in those "private places" where no human eyes see. Retreating to those "private places" such as another city or town where no one knows you, in your locked

Instead of praying to have God "take away" your sexual desires, ask him for the strength to endure and overcome those moments of great temptation.

room, hotel room – places like that, where you can view these things privately.

Amnon's lust became an obsession.

This desire became inflamed and out of control. He had an image of Tamar burned in his mind. He may have used his imagination to visualize Tamar without clothes, or he could have practiced voyeurism - looking at a naked person within the privacy of their dwelling, without them knowing.

Have you ever watched some men whose eyes seem to be undressing a female as she walks by? You can almost tell what they might be thinking. They watch her every move until she is no longer in their view. It is very interesting to watch them in action. They pretend that they are not looking but at times it becomes so obvious. It would not be a far stretch to think that Amnon may have been doing something like this for quite some time.

This obsession seemed out of control, as evidenced by the fact he began to lose weight over the issue. His appetite was no longer what it used to be. He began to suffer from insomnia. All he could think of was Tamar while visualizing what it would be like to be with her in bed. This became more and more obvious as we'll see.

Obsessions can be very dangerous. There are stories of horrific actions that have taken place because of an obsession. As a result of obsessive behavior many people are serving time in prison, families have been disrupted, lives have been lost, careers have been destroyed, businesses have been ruined, and the list goes on and on.

Here are some other words that can be used to describe an obsession.

Infatuation.

Crush.

Preoccupation.

You could say that Amnon had a crush on Tamar. He was infatuated with her. His mind was preoccupied with her. He just could not shake the thoughts or the feelings. The more he thought about her the more intense these feelings became.

There was a news report in 2007 of a former astronaut who drove cross-country, from Texas to Florida, to confront someone who she considered a rival over the affections of another male astronaut (Watson & Stone, 2007). The trip was 950 miles one way.

She was so obsessed with this other male astronaut that she was willing to drive cross-country with the intent of kidnapping her rival, and do bodily harm to her. The police found in her possession a steel mallet, a buck knife with a four inch blade, a BB gun and a map to the her rival's house.

She told the police that she wore diapers so she would not have to stop to use the bathroom. This was how obsessed she was. Did I mention that she was married and had three children? The risks that people will take when they are overcome by obsession are just unfathomable.

Struggling with sexual issues

Amnon was obviously struggling with sexual issues to which most young people, and for that matter some adults, can relate. It is important to note that being sexual i.e. having sexual thoughts and desires, is a natural part of the developmental process.

Some people think that it is wrong and sinful to have these thoughts and desires. Some go to great length trying to suppress these feelings. Some seek out counseling while others pray intensely asking God to take away these feelings. This is especially so when these feelings are at their peak to the point of acting out sexually.

God will not take away those feelings. He does not give something and then take it back. This is a principle that needs to be repeatedly emphasized. Instead of asking God to take away these urges, ask him to give you the strength to be self-controlled. These urges are given so they can be acted upon within the context of marriage. That is the plan of God and the reason behind the feelings.

Imagine with me for a moment of having asked God to take away your sexual urges and He granted your request. You are now married. What do you think your prayer would be at this point? Would you be begging and pleading with God to reverse what he granted? I think you would.

God created us with sexual desires and to have then fulfilled within the context of marriage. Any fulfillment of these desires outside of marriage, from God's standpoint, is sinful. Some people will argue this and try to justify times when it is or should be okay. They will say such things as, "if two people truly love each other then it is okay to have sex". They will also make the argument that the belief of sex being experienced only within the confines of marriage and nowhere else is archaic, old fashioned, unrealistic and no one can expect a person to wait until such time. I'm not sure on what side of the aisle you find yourself on this issue. Since this book is not for the purpose of making the case for God's idea of abstinence until marriage, I'll just say that I would give God, who created sex, credit for knowing what he is talking about. It was and still is, his idea.

It is safe to say that most men and women have experienced some form of sexual struggle. The more common struggles that most men experience – at least the ones that I have spoken to or counseled with, happen to be pornography, lust and masturbation. Pornography tends to take the lead. These struggles may be more intense for some than it is for others.

> *"What you feed, grows; what you starve, dies"*

Some people are successful in handling them while others are not.

If you find yourself struggling, please note that you are not alone even though it may seem as if you are. I too have had my own share of struggles. I sometimes wonder if this is one of the thorns in the flesh, which the Apostle Paul spoke about in 2 Corinthians 12:7b "… so to keep me from becoming proud, I was given a thorn in the flesh, a messenger of Satan to torment me and keep me from becoming proud".

Sometimes these struggles do come about by our own doing. We expose ourselves to situations and experiences that feed or open the door to these struggles. This could be heterosexual or homosexual in nature. An example of this could be exposure to pornographic material whether electronic or print. This imprints an image on the mind, which will be replayed at various times. An appetite has now been birthed for more porn.

As we give place to this appetite, the more it grows. One of the sayings that I use a lot in seminars or in counseling is "what you feed, grows; what you starve, dies." As this pattern develops, the possibility exists that we could become addicted to pornography. This addiction can lead to a plethora of problems in current or future relationships. Was this the case of Amnon? Was he now experiencing the outgrowth of what he had fed? I will let *you* make that conclusion as you read on.

One of the problems that are presented in counseling is the lack of intimacy within the relationship. A wife who finds out her husband is into pornography feels she cannot compete with what her husband is being exposed to. He begins to compare what he is experiencing visually to what is happening sexually in the marriage. He now concludes that his wife is no longer performing to his now newfound level of expectancy. His interest in her dissipates. She sees, feels, and knows it. This creates a problem that affects intimacy. This is just one of the few problems that will be experienced.

Let me hasten to say that not all struggles are self-inflicted, meaning they did not come from one's own choice. Some of these struggles come as a result of sexual violation at an early age. This trauma may have resulted in dominant behaviors or thoughts that are sexual in nature. I have read stories and have also worked with clients who have experienced such trauma from an early age. They begin to behave inappropriately to others, thinking that their behavior is normal. An example of this is a child who has been molested and begins to act out sexually around other children without realizing the ramifications of such. That child begins to think that this is the way to gain acceptance, feel good about self, or punish self for being "bad." They may see themselves as "bad" because of what happened to them or because of what their perpetrator may have told them.

I remember reading a story of a psychologist who was working with a child who was sexually abused for many years. When he first met her and began to work with her, one of the first things she did was to walk over to him, sat on his lap, and tried to reach down and unbutton his pants. The psychologist reacted quickly to this without reprimanding the child, but firmly and lovingly removed her from his lap. This was a "red-flag" for him as to what her problems might be.

In some instances, a child who has been molested by someone of the same sex, may think that this is what his or her future sexual experience should be. As a result, he or she may end up pursuing same sex relationships. This is not always true in every case but it does in some cases. The same is true for female-to-female sexual assault. Again, this is just a generality and not a scientific prediction. I can almost hear the voices of those who would argue that I am making the case to excuse people's behavior as something they cannot help because of what happened to them. Let me say that I think people are always responsible for their actions but sometimes the reason for their behavior is directly related to past trauma and should be factored in.

These issues can be very sensitive in nature and difficult to talk about. Like it was for me, so it is for many people. They do not want to talk about it. It is too painful. This is where a trusted counselor, spiritual leader, or mentor, can be helpful in talking about these and other issues.

If you are a parent of a child who is of age to understand sexual issues, let me impress on you the importance of talking with him or her about such matters. Do not assume they are too young to have this kind of discussion and do not leave this very important discussion to others. If you don't talk with your child about this sensitive matter, someone else will.

Become informed so that you can have an educated discussion with them. You could talk with your spiritual leader or another professional, about how to approach the subject. You may want to ask if some of what you are observing are normal and / or age appropriate. Are there any signs or behaviors that require closer scrutiny than others, and if there are, what are they? One of the things that I tell parents is that they should try not to react or act shocked, at their child's behavior or statements, but to seize the moment and not have a knee-jerk reaction. By seizing the moment I mean to either use it as a teachable or an exploratory moment.

An example of this might be a teen saying that they are feeling pressured to have sex because all of their friends are doing it. In this scenario, the first thing is to calmly ask them to tell you more about the pressure. The following questions may be use to illicit conversation.

- How much pressure?
- How frequent is it?
- When do they feel it most?
- How are they dealing with it?
- How could you help them?

You are trying to get a better grasp on what might be going on in their mind and possibly gauge where they are in relation to the pressure they described. This would be categorized as a teachable and exploratory moment. This is just one of the ways your spiritual leader or another professional may be helpful. The key ingredient is to build a relationship with your child so that you can have this kind of discussion with them.

Dealing with temptation

None of us can say we have never been tempted; even Jesus was tempted. The scripture says in Hebrews 4:15 (NLT), that Jesus "faced all of the same temptations we do, yet he did not sin." In Matthew 4:1-4, you can read where Jesus came under incredible temptation, which he overcame. He was very vulnerable when he faced his temptations. These are the times when we are more apt to succumb to our temptation. We are always tempted in areas of our weakness. The passage says he was very hungry after not eating for forty days. He was fasting, going without food, as a way of disciplining the body and clearing the mind. Jesus used this time to focus entirely on God the Father.

> *All of us have dealt with temptation. Have you ever noticed that we never get tempted to do the right thing? We are tempted to satisfy our desires in all the wrong ways or at the wrong time.*

The devil seized this opportunity to tempt him with food. This is what Jesus desired after forty days without eating. So it makes sense that food is what he would use. The Devil will use the thing that you and I desire the most to tempt us. When the food temptation did not work, he attempted to use pride. When that did not work, he made one last effort in offering Jesus material possessions. This also did not work, so he took a break to regroup and come back at a later date. This is similar to how we are tempted. We may overcome our temptation today, but don't ever become too comfortable thinking that we have made it, because the Devil is coming back again.

Some people will refer to temptation as something God is using to make them stronger or to test their faith. This is an erroneous thinking. The Bible says clearly that "God is never tempted to do wrong, and he never tempts anyone else either. Temptation comes from the lure of our own evil desires. These evil desires lead to evil actions, and evil actions lead to death. So don't be misled …." James 1:13b-16a.

Temptation also comes from the Devil. He will make suggestions to us that offer temporary satisfaction, but in the end it leads to our hurt. Always. Because he is the father of all lies (John 8:44), he cannot ever offer us something that would be helpful to us in the long run. Every thing he offers is 100% untrue. No truth is in him.

Most men I know are moved mostly by what they see and what they see arouses these desires. This is called temptation or according to one pastor, "it is the pull of the skin away from God." Amnon was experiencing incredible temptation as he lusted after Tamar. He became sexually aroused as a result of this.

Simply looking extensively at someone to whom we are attracted, a nude or partially nude body that is in print or video format, can lead to sexual arousal. That is one of the reasons, if not the main reason, why pornography, which has the ability to create such arousals, is a multi-billion dollar industry.

When we combine this with our thought process, we become sexually aroused. This arousal is what gets us in trouble. Not only does it lead to sexual thoughts, but also to sexual intercourse and/or masturbation. The topic of masturbation can be very controversial with some people saying it is okay, while others saying it is not. This is something you will need to talk through with a godly, non-judgmental, and trustworthy individual.

Sexual thoughts can be quite normal within certain contexts. Thoughts of any kind are hard to block from our minds. They come at us from various sources. You may not be able to stop the thought, but you have the power over what you do with that thought. An analogy I have heard numerous times in reference to thoughts, is that "you can't stop the birds from flying over your head, but you sure can stop them from landing and making their nest on your head." So it is with your thoughts.

Having said that, we must then ask ourselves how can we reconcile the teachings of Jesus, which states that to even look at a woman lustfully is tantamount to the act of sexual sin - adultery. Matthew 5:28 (NLT), "But I say, anyone who even looks at a woman with lust in his eye has already committed adultery with her in his heart."

I'll be brief in saying Jesus simply means that when we look and continuously stare at a woman – "undress" her with our eyes, we have committed adultery. The sexual act has already taken place within our minds.

Some people, when they read this, feel like they might as well not stop at the thought if they are already guilty for having lusted. Those who would hold to this thought fail to understand that the purpose of this teaching is to help us with our thought life. It's not just the glance or the one-time look. It is the constant staring and bringing into the equation, our vivid imagination. Especially for us guys, it's almost impossible to not look. We are more visual and easily stimulated. It is not just the look that makes it adultery; it is the fixation.

As you can see this topic can become rather extensive in trying to explain some of its concepts. This is not the purpose of this writing so forgive me if I don't go as deep as you would like.

Amnon now had a choice and a decision to make, as to what to do with the temptation he was now experiencing.

CHAPTER FOUR

Love Requires Words and Actions

4b "So Amnon told him, "I am in love with Tamar, Absalom's sister

Amnon professed to love Tamar. It was this "love" for her that triggered what became his obsession. Did he really love her? Was this true love? What is love?

Have you ever had someone profess to love you but you found out after a while that they really did not? What really is love? Is love a feeling? Is love an action?

Explaining 'Love'

Explaining what 'love' means can be at times difficult, but at least we have the perfect example of what that looks like as demonstrated by our heavenly Father.

The Bible says in Romans 5:8 that God demonstrated or showed his love for us by sending his son, Jesus Christ, to die for us on the cross. That is the ultimate love. No one has ever loved as he has.

> *Love protects, nourishes, and cherishes*

Whenever someone says that they love you, here are some qualities that serve as an excellent guideline for you to judge that declaration. 1 Corinthians 13:1-7 provides the qualities that you should be looking for:

- *Love is patient and kind.*
- *Love is not jealous, boastful, proud or rude.*
- *It does not demand its own way.*
- *It is not irritable.*
- *It keeps no record of being wronged.*
- *It does not rejoice about injustice.*
- *But rejoices whenever the truth wins out.*
- *Love never gives up,*

- *Never loses faith,*
- *Is always hopeful,*
- *And endures through every circumstance.*

You could use the above definition to decide whether someone really loves you. They might not be perfect in all of them, but they should have some visible traits of most of them. You could substitute the word love with the name of the person you are thinking of. See how they stack up. If there are more "no's" than "yes," then you really need to reconsider if it is true love that you are experiencing.

If you are in a relationship where you are feeling pressured by your partner to do something that you don't want to do, then that person has no respect for you, doesn't care about you, your feelings or your wishes, and does not have your best interest at heart. They are only about themselves. It doesn't matter how handsome or beautiful they are. They want to use you to their own selfish end.

In the same way, use the test on the previous page to answer the question of love for yourself. How do you know if he or she really loves you? Is it by what they say or by what they do?

You will be able to determine which of the "L" words (love or lust) they are expressing towards you. Love says, "I'll wait 5 years." Lust says, "I can't wait five minutes." Love protects, nourishes, and cherishes.

It is quite easy for one person to tell another that they love them but not mean it. It doesn't take much effort to do that. Words can be cheap.

Some guys will tell females how much they love them and how much they mean to them. They will then follow up within the same context or sometime soon after, by requesting sex.

These guys know how to skillfully articulate, their request. It will be done in the most charming and convincing way possible. They will have already figured out the fact that females need love. They have taken the time to learn by observing and will offer them so-called love to get sex. Some females, will in turn give sex just to get love. The sad part is that they will lose the most from this exchange. The only person who comes away getting what they want, is the guy.

Maybe you did not experience true love if any at all, from your parent or parents, especially your dad. Your emotional tank is empty. It needs to be filled. Every one of us has a need for love.

Several years ago I heard a public speech where the speaker made the following statement, "Bad love is better than no love." He also quoted this statement from C.S. Lewis, "the human appetite will not tolerate being ignored. You'll satisfy it rightly or wrongly. It won't go away."

Solomon puts it this way, "a person who is full refuses honey, but even bitter food tastes sweet to the hungry." (Proverbs 27:7) In other words, if you are hungry for love, you will settle for whatever kind you can get even if it is bad love. This is where most mistakes are made, but also where it is most important to remind yourself that God loves you and has a plan for your life and this is surely not it. I acknowledge that this is easier said than done but it is still the fact. If you can wrap your mind around this, it could make all the difference in your world.

My Story

I grew up in a household where I knew that my dad and mom loved me. It was mostly evident by what they did for us as children.

As I look back on my childhood, I have for the last several years struggled to remember a time that my dad said these words to me, "I love you!" I want to make it clear that I *just can't remember that being done*! If he did, it must have been so minimal that it just did not make an impact on me. I have asked most of my siblings to see if they could remember a time that our dad ever said those words to them.

He, (my dad), was a very stereotypical "old school" dad. Men for the most part, and here I am speaking in general terms, are not very expressive in the area of emotions. He grew up in an era when men were not supposed to cry. Crying was a sign of weakness. I'm sure there are still areas of the world where this kind of thinking is still being instilled in the minds of little boys.

Growing up, I remember hearing words like "don't cry, its going to be alright!" or "big boys don't cry" or "you are a boy so 'tuff it out!" These statements were made in reference to an experience I might have had from falling or being involved in a fight, etc.

When someone says, "it's going to be alright," my question is, "how do they know?" Can they see in the future? Do they know how I feel?

This was the kind of world my dad grew up in. Showing affection was not one of his strengths. This seems to be true for most men (again speaking in generality), who were from his era, and more prevalent among islanders (people from the island are referred to as islanders). As someone from the island of Jamaica, West Indies, who have witnessed and experienced this, I believe I can make such a broad statement. That was my dad's world.

To be fair to him, he grew up without a dad. His dad died at an early age. As the eldest child, he had to take on the role of being the provider within the home. This was one of the factors, which prevented him from completing high school.

In addition to not recalling a time hearing my dad saying to me "I love you", I cannot recall hearing him say it to my mom. This was also true of him expressing his affection to her publicly. I do admit that this was again one of those things that were not seen frequently between husband and wife, within our culture. I don't remember seeing a whole lot of that.

Maybe my dad grew up not hearing those words from his mom and obviously not from his father who died at an early age. He could not give what he did not have. I now realize that, even more so as a Family Therapist.

Not having heard those words while growing up played a big part in my life. I found it hard to do the same. I could make an effort initially but once I became comfortable or familiar in certain settings, I defaulted to the status quo. I realized that I did not have much of a problem saying that when I was in the "hunt" for a relationship with someone of the opposite sex. I had an ulterior motive so I made the effort. The first half of the saying "guys give girls love to have sex, and girls give sex to have love," described me. I would do that a lot during my "wild and crazy" youthful days - sowing wild oats as they say. Something I am not proud of, but I cannot change it.

My wife has been very helpful in this area. She is a very affectionate person so she relates to me in an affectionate manner, exercising much patience with me. I try my best to be cooperative for more reasons than one.

The main reason is the decision I made before getting married and having children. I wanted to make sure they did not have to wonder if their dad loved them. I make it a regular practice to tell them. I also do that with my wife, though not as much as she would like, and I would agree with her on that. I still have to be intentional about saying it. I'm still a work in progress.

I have come to the realization that love is both doing something for someone, and verbally letting him or her know as well. It is not one without the other. They go hand in hand. This you will see with Amnon who professed his love for Tamar. He verbally communicated it but did he mean it?

Even though love is more about doing than it is about saying, it still requires both. There needs to be a balance.

Here are questions you need to honestly ask yourself as you ponder if you are being loved: How is this person seeking to *protect* me and *provide* for me?

If I was to base love on these two fundamental qualities of protection and provision, my dad loved me hands down. He provided a place for us to live, clothes to wear, a good education, food to eat (I never went to bed hungry), good moral and religious upbringing, etc. Based on that I would say he loved me.

On the other hand, I could get technical and say he failed to provide me with a model for healthy relationship. We never had a close relationship that most, if not all boys wish to have with their father. He did not teach me about what it meant to grow up as a young man - such things as puberty and what happens during that time, sex, how to choose a mate, and so on. Most of this I had to learn on the "streets." What I learned was surely not what he wanted me to learn, but it was too late.

I wished I had the kind of communication between father and son where I could have talked about anything. Unfortunately that was not the case. Most children would appreciate knowing they can talk with their parents about these topics.

Maybe this was true of Amnon. His dad – David, may not have been involved in his life consistently. That was more the mother's role in his culture. Unconditional love may not have been something he grew up understanding from his dad. As it was for me, he may have longed for his father's affection and attention.

Parents, let me encourage you to talk with your children. Build a relationship with them. Tell them you love them on a regular basis.

Even though telling someone that you love him or her can be said without much thought or meaning, it is still important. It can become the fuel to get the engine of changed behavior started, where the journey of new experiences can begin. Once someone is fulfilling the two foundational qualities - provision and protection, then the verbalizing of love – the third component, will be more meaningful; it's more believable.

These are two of the foundational qualities of love. If someone is not seeking to protect or provide for you, then you should question whether he or she truly loves you.

How could Amnon have shown love towards Tamar?

He could do this by looking out for her overall wellbeing: not take advantage of her, defend her against others, and treat her as the "weaker vessel."

I am very aware that some women may feel offended or be upset that I would use the term "weaker vessel." For those who would, let me hastily say that this is in no way referring to her abilities but to the fact that she was made to be cared for. It is a term that the Bible uses to make the point that husbands treat their wives delicately (1 Pet. 3:7). Most women I know would prefer to be cared for and if they had a vote on the matter, would vote this way every time.

One of the main complaints that I hear from female clients, who come into my office for marriage or couples counseling, is that he - meaning the husband or husband to be - doesn't care. This is based upon what the expectations were going into the relationship. The general thought is if he cared he would do this or that without me having to tell him. However, a thought unexpressed is a thought unfulfilled. This could easily be remedied by a change in communication that includes sharing hopes, expectations, wishes and dreams.

You may recall being at a birthday party where the person who was celebrating his or her birthday, was asked to make a wish before he or she blew out the candle. However, it was supposed to be a silent wish. No one was supposed to know what he or she was wishing for.

As simple and innocent as this "game" was, it could have lasting effects. This child could be terribly disappointed if what they were wishing for did not become a reality and more so if the opposite happened. That child could grow up having a complex in the area of trust.

What if that child had shared that wish? The likelihood of it becoming a reality would be exponentially increased.

That is what happens in many relationships. One or both of the partners have these "silent wishes" but never expresses them hoping that his or her partner would know and fulfill them. When it doesn't happen, it creates conflict.

Through re-education, dedication, and hard work, issues of this sort can be resolved.

As this story unfolds, you will be able to answer the following questions about Amnon: Was he in love with Tamar or in lust with her? Did he seek to protect her? Was he nourishing or cherishing of her? Was he patient and kind? Was he demanding his own way?

CHAPTER FIVE

Be Careful WHOM You Go To For Advice!

2 Amnon became so obsessed with Tamar that he became ill. She was a virgin, and it seemed impossible that he could ever fulfill his love for her. 3 "Now Amnon had a very crafty friend -- his cousin Jonadab. He was the son of David's brother Shimea. 4 One day Jonadab said to Amnon, "What's the trouble? Why should the son of a king look so dejected morning after morning? "So Amnon told him, "I am in love with Tamar, Absalom's sister 5 "Well," Jonadab said, "I'll tell you what to do. Go back to bed and pretend you are sick. When your father comes to see you, ask him to let Tamar come and prepare some food for you. Tell him you'll feel better if she feeds you 6 So Amnon pretended to be sick. And when the king came to see him, Amnon asked him, "Please let Tamar come to take care of me and cook something for me to eat."

Amnon could take it no more. His frustration level was at the breaking point. This was too much for him. He had to do something. He finally contacted his cousin Jonadab, to request a face-to-face meeting.

He could not think of a better person to call than his cousin, Jonadab. He had to talk to someone whom he could trust. Someone who he thought might understand what he was feeling. No electronic medium would suffice. It had to be face to face. He wanted to see Jonadab's reaction to what he had to share. This was too important to him.

Jonadab finally came to see Amnon.

Amnon immediately met him at the door as soon as he arrived. He did not even allow him to enter.

"Man, thanks for coming," he hurriedly said. "I have been waiting for you to get here. We need to talk. I don't want to do it here, so come with me."

Jonadab's mind began to wonder what this could be about. Was this in response to the comment he had made to Amnon about how he was looking sad and depressed or was it in response to something he did but was not aware.

Jonadab was a very shrewd guy. He was known as a ladies' man. He was one of the most popular guys on campus and the envy of many of his male counterparts. He did not seem to have a problem with girls. He may have been wondering if he had made a misstep along the way involving Amnon. These may have been some of his thoughts:

Am I in trouble?

Is this a set-up?

Is this just between him and me?

Is he planning something?

Is my suspicion of why I thought he wants to see me, about to become a reality?

Have you ever had someone send you a message requesting to see you? Your thoughts run wild especially if you are guilty of something. You begin to wonder what you may have done. All the craziest thoughts come rushing to your mind.

Jonadab quickly brought his mind into focus so that Amnon would not see the concern he was having.

"What's up? Man, you look so depressed. What's going on with you?" Jonadab said in as controlled a manner as he possibly could. "It seems like you haven't had much sleep lately. Are you feeling well? It looks like you have lost weight"

"Its nothing. I'm good. I'm all right. Just taking it easy. What's up with you?" Amnon tried his best to not sound like he really had a burning issue on which he wanted Jonadab's opinion.

"C'mon man, who are you fooling? You know it's not alright." Jonadab said pausing for a moment. "You can tell me. I'm your cousin, remember; your favorite cousin. I won't tell anyone. You can trust me. You can be real with me."

Amnon took a deep breath and then pulled Jonadab to the side where no one else could overhear their conversation. "Okay. Okay. I'm going to level with you. Promise me you won't tell anyone. Okay?"

Amnon waited for a confirmation from Jonadab. Once he felt comfortable with the response, he continued. "Man, this is crazy. You won't believe it. You know my half-brother Absalom's sister Tamar — right?" Jonadab nodded with a suspicious look on his face. "Well I think I'm in love with her. I want her. I'm obsessed with her. Isn't that crazy? Does that make sense?"

Jonadab took a deep breath and tried very hard not to act shocked. He wanted to take Amnon seriously. After regaining his composure, he said, "Dude, you must be kidding, right? This is a joke. Are you serious?"

"I'm really serious. This is not a joke."

Jonadab, seeing the look on Amnon's face was convinced that he was very serious.

As they continued their stroll, they came upon a leftover stump from a huge tree. Amnon suggested that they sit for a while. They both sat down. Jonadab reached down and picked up a dried branch that was lying close by. He began to tap it on the ground to break the eerie silence.

After a few minutes he spoke up. "Here's my suggestion. Don't go to school tomorrow. Call in sick to work. When your dad finds out that you did not go to school or work, he will want to know why. When he comes to see you, tell him that you aren't feeling well and that you would like Tamar to make you a special meal. Make up a story about the meal and why you are making this request."

Amnon allowed Jonadab's suggestion to sink in, and then responded, "Are you serious. Do you think that will work?"

"It's worth a try unless you have a better idea. You asked me for my opinion, and I'm just saying —"

"Humph. Okay, I think I will do that", Amnon said as he abruptly interrupted Jonadab. "At this point I'm open to any ideas. I just hope dad will go for it. Man, I'm nervous." With that said, as he took a deep breath and slowly exhaled.

After a few moments of silence, they made their way back to Amnon's house. Not much was said as they walked. It was an awkward moment for both of them.

Jonadab wished Amnon all the best as they parted ways.

Amnon had a lot on his mind as he made his way to his room, lay on his bed, and began to think of his next move. It seemed like eternity. He tossed and turned trying to figure out how to convince his dad to allow Tamar to come to his house. What if he said no? What if he did not buy the story? Then what?

What should I be doing when he comes?

Where should I be sitting or should I be lying down?

How should I begin the conversation?

When should I send for him?

These were just a few of the questions with which he wrestled. There was no room for error. Every area that he could possibly think of had to be covered, including his dad's possible response.

Have you ever had to weigh a very difficult decision? Do you remember how you felt within? The churning within your stomach! The sleepless nights! Having little or no-appetite! Do you remember those days? You might be having one of those vivid memories right now as you read this chapter. If so, you may be able to identify with what Amnon more than likely was feeling.

I remember how long it took for me to ask my father and mother-in-law for permission to marry their daughter. It took me weeks to build enough courage to ask them. I would go over in my mind all the questions that I would ask and the possible responses I would get. What if they said no? What if they did not agree? What would I do? Thankfully they said yes. What a relief! Amnon could have been wrestling with similar thoughts.

After hours of rehearsal he eventually mustered up the courage to send for his dad. He rehearsed where he would be when his dad arrived, how he would sound, and what facial expression he would have. He felt that he was now comfortable with his rehearsal.

He called one of his servants and relayed the message for his dad informing him of his sickness. He was not sure if his dad would actually come and see him. No time can be as long as when you are anxiously awaiting a very important response. Amnon felt very restless as he awaited the reply.

When I took one of my exams to become licensed as a Marriage and Family Therapist in the State of Florida, I had to wait almost a month for the results. In the days of electronics, I really don't see why it had to take that long, especially since I did it electronically.

Everyday that went by, my mind was on the results of the exam. People would ask me how I felt I did. In wanting to downplay it, I would say something to the effect that I think I did okay. I did not want to portray a level of confidence and then only to find out that I failed. This is a pass or fail exam. What made matters worse was that this was my third attempt at it. I eventually passed it.

Once I found out that I did, I was so excited. For a moment, I thought it was not real. I was in a state of shock, not believing what I saw. My wife and family were so excited for me. It was a great feeling. I could finally exhale. Have you ever had such an experience?

Amnon is now where I was; he was holding his breath waiting his turn to exhale. Until his dad showed up and he was able to make his Oscar-like presentation, he could not yet exhale. This wait probably seemed like an eternity.

Choosing The Right Adviser

As I think about Amnon's choice of an adviser, I wonder why he chose Jonadab as his 'go-to' person. Was he Amnon's closest friend? Was it because he was the most popular guy on campus? Was it because he was his cousin? Was it because he and Amnon were very much like-minded?

Whatever the reason, Amnon chose him.

How do you choose your advisers? Would you have chosen a Jonadab-type?

Most times, we go to those with whom we already have a close relationship. But is that a good idea when you have a very important or major decision to make?

Jonadab's advice is not surprising. It seems to fit well with his character. He was very crafty, self-centered, and shrewd. It seems that no matter what he said, Amnon would do because of how desperate he was.

Jonadab wasn't thinking about what this might do to Amnon's family and most importantly, to Tamar. He was quick to give Amnon this advice knowing very well that he was not the one who would have to live with the consequences of his actions.

One of the lessons we could learn here is that not everyone has our best interest at heart. We need to be careful from who we take advice or counsel. The Bible specifically says in Psalm 1:1 (KJV), "Blessed is the man that walketh not in the counsel of the ungodly, nor standeth in the way of sinners, nor sitteth in the seat of the scornful." The word "walketh" simply means, "taking the advice of."

The meaning of the verse indicates that a person is blessed when he or she chooses not to take ungodly advice or counsel.

Some people give advice with hidden motives. Sometimes they have something to gain from the advice that they are giving. Isn't it interesting that some do not follow their own advice?

A good rule of thumb is to look at the lives of those from whom you are seeking advice. Are their lives in order? Are they being successful by following their own advice? These are just a couple questions to ask yourself about those from whom you are seeking advice.

A humorous story, which may have had some exaggeration, was told by one of my favorite speakers – Zig Ziglar. He shared about a celebrity being interviewed on how to keep a husband. She began her discourse about what works and what doesn't. This woman has had three failed marriages. Zig described her as having rice marks on her face from the amount of marriages she's been through. There was a time, as the bride and groom exited the church, people would line up on both sides creating an aisle for them through which to walk. As the couple walked through the newly created aisle, the people would throw rice at them. Throwing rice was symbolic of fertility. It is more of an American tradition where well-wishers would throw seeds whether birdseeds or rice, wishing a prosperous union for the couple.

Obviously this woman whose face has "rice marks" is not the expert on keeping a husband. She would not be the most qualified person to ask about how to keep a husband.

Unfortunately, we tend to go to our friends for such advice, without taking into consideration their life experiences or by asking ourselves if they are further along in their life's journey than we are.

Amnon sought out someone who had a questionable reputation. Someone whom you would say had very low morals and values.

One of the sayings I grew up hearing, which you probably did as well was, "birds of a feather flock together" and "show me your friends and I'll tell you who you are."

Solomon gave us this word of wisdom: "Walk with the wise and become wise, associate with fools and get in trouble" (Proverbs 13:20). One of the prophets of old made the following statement: "Can two walk together unless they are in agreement?" (Amos 3:3).

Amnon definitely would not have sought out the advice of someone who would not have given him the answer he wanted. This is the approach that many people use when seeking advice. They are seeking for someone to agree with them. How do you seek after advice? Do you go to your spiritual leader, parent, an adult you can trust, or do you only go to your friends – your peers?

Here are some thoughts from Andy Stanley, Sr. Pastor of Northpoint Community Church in Atlanta,

Georgia, on how to choose the right people to go for advice.

- *Choose someone who has nothing to lose by telling you the truth. These people are less concerned about the friendship than they are about you - the friend.*
- *Choose someone who is at a place in life that you want to be in the future. They have much more experience than you and are more successful at life than you.*
- *Choose someone who has a good reputation and is a person of good character.*
- *Choose to listen to a close adviser as well as an unbiased "counselor". Therefore, ask more than one person.*

Here are three questions that you can ask of a trusted adviser.

- *Are any of the options outside the boundaries of scriptures as far as you know?*
- *Based on what you know about me or have learned about me, what do you think I should do?*
- *If you were me, what would you do?*

As a counselor, one of the things I seek *not* to do is to give advice to my clients - tell them what to do. I have been taught and have come to realize that people need to make their own decision on a matter and take responsibility for their actions.

It is very important to help people look at different options, and then let them choose which they think would work best for them and their present situation.

It is easy for me to tell someone what to do, when I am not the one living with the consequences of the actions. They are the ones who are the experts on their lives. They know what would work best for them in their present situation.

This does not mean that they are not challenged to stretch themselves and realize that there are times they may have to accept negative consequences, for the good of self, family, or society. This may be the price to pay.

I don't think that Amnon thought this through. He was acting impulsively. This describes a lot of younger people today who act without thinking things through.

There was a story reported on KOMO News in Seattle, of a teen girl and a young adult male who were playing a game called Strip-Me on an over pass. This game included trying to hit the top of vehicles with small rocks, as they passed below. Whoever missed had to take off one piece of clothing. The guy was obviously winning judging by who had most of their clothes off when the cops arrived. One of the rocks broke the windshield of a lady's car causing injury. The cops were called. They were arrested.

They did not know that street cameras were capturing their activities. On the videotape you could see them trying to grab their clothes - mostly hers, and hurriedly getting dressed. According to KOMO News, the teen girl was asked by one of the officers why she would do such a thing. Her remarks were atypical, "I don't know. I wasn't thinking." Sounds familiar?

Apparently this girl was like most teenagers or young adults, who do not think things through before they act. It's act now; think later.

This is frustrating to many parents and other adults, who have a hard time wondering why teenagers are so impulsive, irrational, and temperamental. Sometimes they seem to have a Jekyll and Hype personality. They are one way today and another tomorrow. It's as if they have split personalities.

Why are they like this you ask? They are like this because they are still in the process of learning and trying to understand life. They are not at the point yet where the processing center of the brain - prefrontal cortex, is fully developed. They react mostly from the raw emotions area of the brain - the limbic system or impulse area.

This is why much patience, grace, mercy, love, and forgiveness has to be measured out even when it is the last thing you as a parent, mentor, or other adult want to give. Max Lucado says, "Patience is the red carpet on which grace walks".

These are the individuals that are sought out for expert advice by some of their peers. You ask the question, how wise will their advice be? They do not have the life experience or the learning experience to give the most helpful and meaningful advice.

This does not mean that every adult gives great advice. I have heard advice given by some adults that made me wonder if it was an adult who was really the one speaking.

Therefore, going to someone for advice who doesn't have the maturity to think things through or to think about the long-term impact of one's decision, can be dangerous. This is what we see when it came to the advice Jonadab gave to Amnon.

Not only is it advisable to refrain from seeking advice from someone who is not qualified, it is also a good idea to have face to face communication on matters of importance. If there is one thing that we could say that Amnon did right, it was to request a face-to-face meeting with Jonadab.

Face to face is always best

One valuable lesson I have learned is that trying to communicate something of importance electronically can easily be misinterpreted or misunderstood. If or when it does, it sometimes takes a long time to try and clear up any misunderstanding.

This is one of the reasons I do not recommend the use of electronic media to communicate important pieces of information *unless* it is going to be read to the intended person or be read in your presence. I know that there are times when this is the only way to communicate, which leaves you with no other choice.

People are always communicating

Some people have also told me that writing out their thoughts, helps them think through what they need to say, which protects them from saying something they would later regret.

I can see this being the method of choice especially when the person with whom you are communicating constantly interrupts. It is easy to lose your train of thought and sometimes the constant interruption shuts down conversation. This can lead to frustration, resentment, and possibly bitterness.

Communication problems are another reason many couples come to me for counseling. I always ask what that means to them, because communication means different things to different people.

You are reading what *I* am communicating - my thoughts and insights on Tamar's story. I am currently using one of the three forms of communication. The other two are verbal (speaking) and non-verbal (actions). Communication is always taking place.

Another of the many complaints I hear mostly from my clients who are presenting with relational problems, is that their partner doesn't want to communicate with them. What they are really saying is that this person doesn't want to talk to them. How would they know that the other person doesn't want to talk if they are not talking? Technically, they *did* communicate — non-verbally.

To really know what a person is possibly thinking or feeling, having a face-to-face meeting is the preferred way of communication. A person's body language and tone of voice is a good indicator as to how he or she is processing what has been said. Unfortunately we are living in a time when more and more communication is taking place via the social media such as Facebook, Twitter, Email, etc. This form of communication is cancelling out one of the most important pieces of communication, the non-verbal.

Most young people today are not developing the skill-sets around mood, tone, and words. They are not able to make the connection. They are unable to detect when someone is sending a message through facial expression or body positioning. This puts them at a disadvantage when physically interacting.

This is one area for which we have to give Amnon credit. He knew the importance of face-to-face communication.

He now waited patiently for his dad's arrival.

CHAPTER SIX

Not Everyone Thinks The Same

6b And when the king came to see him, Amnon asked him, "Please let Tamar come to take care of me and cook something for me to eat." 7 So David agreed and sent Tamar to Amnon's house to prepare some food for him

David eventually showed up at his son's - Amnon's door. Upon his father's entrance, Amnon began the rehearsed presentation of his illness and his need to have his sister Tamar come and cook for him.

Walking into the room, David said, "Hey son, I heard you weren't feeling well. How are you now? What do you think is wrong?"

Amnon, groaning as if he was in pain, and trying to look convincing, slowly, and with barely a whisper said to his dad, "I don't know what is wrong. Just not feeling well. It has been going on for a couple of days. I tried to ignore it, but somehow it seems to have gotten worse. Oh dad. Ouch."

With a concerned look on his face, David said to Amnon, "Do you think we should get you to the doctor?"

Without any hesitation, Amnon quickly responded, "Oh no dad, I think if I rest and have some of Tamar's special food that she makes, I will be okay. You know that special stew she cooks up; it might make me feel better."

"Okay, let's try that and see what happens. If you don't feel better, then we'll go to the doctor. Sounds good?"

"Yeah dad, that sounds good. Ouch!"

As David got up to leave he said, "I'm going to send her to cook the food here so she can keep an eye on you to make sure you are okay."

"Okay dad. Thanks"

Amnon breathed a sigh of relief as soon as his dad walked out the door. In all appearance, he had convinced him. Now his heart began to pick up pace as he had to change emotional gears in anticipation of Tamar's visit.

For Amnon, another hurdle was crossed. "So far so good" he is thinking to himself.

He was unmoved (unfazed) even after this exchange with his dad. No changing of his mind. His mind was made up. He suppressed every emotion that would possibly interfere with his plans. A person who is bent on doing what his or her mind is made up to do, will allow nothing or no one to stop them.

Having no reason to suspect Amnon, David went back to his house and called for his daughter - Tamar.

"Tamar!" David shouted down the hallway of the house.

"Yes dad," Tamar answered sleepily as she was trying to take a nap.

"Come here honey."

"Okay, dad, give me a few minutes," she responded as she tried to get herself together.

Tamar, walking into the room where her dad was, said "Hey dad, what's up?"

"Your brother Amnon is sick in bed. He did not go to school or to work today. Would you go to his house and make some food for him. He's asking for that special meal that you make; you know that special stew"

"You mean the one I made when you were sick?" asked Tamar quizzically.

"Yes, that one."

Tamar, wanting to please her dad, responded, "Okay dad. No problem"

Tamar went and got all the necessary ingredients and headed off to her brother's house. It was just a few yards away from where she lived.

Tamar could have protested that she was asked to fulfill such a request. There is no evidence that she did.

This doesn't mean that she did not. Inwardly, she may have been protesting. However, she wanted to please her dad.

Have you ever been asked to do something by someone to whom you did not really want to say no or just have a hard time saying no? Yet as you proceed to fulfill the request or while fulfilling it, you are "kicking" yourself on the inside. Come on, be honest. You know you have. I think almost all of us have had such an experience.

Despite any misgivings, she eventually went to Amnon's home.

What seemed to be like an eternity for Amnon was about to end. Tamar greeted those who were in the house as she made her way to the kitchen area. She did not waste anytime to begin preparing the meal. She quickly began to unpack all the necessary ingredients she had brought with her. She was a very organized person who wanted everything lay out before she began.

She engaged Amnon in small talk while she immersed herself in the preparation of the meal. She also wanted to get this over as soon as possible so that she could get back to what she was doing and the plans she had for the remainder of the day.

As Amnon watched her preparing the meal, he began to burn with lust. His body went into convulsion. He immediately told his servants to leave them alone together so he could have a "brother-sister" time. Tamar would now take over. They promptly complied.

The servants left.

Tamar thought it was a bit strange that Amnon would make such a request, but did not see any need to question it or think too much about it. She wanted to get the stew finished as quickly as she could, for her brother who was sick. Cooking the meal and having him feeling better was a priority for her. Too bad Amnon wasn't thinking about her welfare in return.

She engaged him once again in conversation. "I'm sorry to hear that you are sick. How are you feeling now? Dad told me that I was to come and make that special meal for you - you know, the one that helped him get over his illness the last time he was sick."

She, like her dad, had no reason to suspect Amnon in his deceptive scheme. She was like a lamb led to the slaughter. She had no idea that she was not going to leave her brother's house the same way she went in.

No reason to suspect

The name Amnon means "faithful." His dad gave him that name in memory of the event(s) surrounding his birth or simply thoughts of God's faithfulness to him. Why would he be suspicious of his "faithful" son? Why would he think that "faithful Amnon" would be lying or deceiving him? He could think of no reason to be suspicious.

Tamar had no reason to suspect Amnon. He was her older brother. He was the one who had the responsibility of taking care of the family should something happen to her dad.

Asking to have some of the special stew, seemed like an innocent request. Why would anyone be suspicious of that? Amnon may not have given anyone of his family members a reason to doubt him. One of my mottos is: "give a person the benefit of the doubt unless there are clear reasons not to."

It's interesting how children who have at least one parent in common can be so totally different. As a matter of fact it happens even when they are of the same parents. Why is this so? Is there more to a person than just his or her biological makeup? Genetics? Are they also products of their environment – the experiences they had in growing up?

Even when both children are from the same parents and grow up within the same home, there is no guarantee that they will end up sharing similar values and morals even though they were all taught them. I know there are arguments for and against these theories and I'm sure you know of someone whose actions blow these theories out of the "water." Again, there is no guarantee.

What was going through Amnon's mind at this time? Was he re-thinking his plan? Was he thinking that this was *his* sister? Did he care about Tamar's future and what this would mean for her?

Amnon may have been too much into himself to even have such thoughts. Thinking about others and their welfare was not one of his strong points. Do you know anyone like that?

The Importance of Being Pure

Tamar being a virgin, was a very big thing culturally, for the women of that society. To not be a virgin when you get married would be shameful and not to mention the amount of questions that would have to be answered.

Some women chose not to get married to avoid such scrutiny. Pre-arranged marriages were very common. Parents would arrange the marriage of their children once they had reached what would be considered the "age-of-marriage."

"Age-of-marriage" would be around eleven or twelve - approximately the age of puberty. In the Jewish culture to which Tamar belonged, there are celebrations marking transition into adulthood. For the girls it's called a Bat Mitzvah and Bar Mitzvah for the boys.

Even though this arrangement was made at this age, the actual ceremony would take place at a future time. However during this time the couple would be considered married. In the western world, we would consider this an engagement.

If a girl lost her virginity and kept it a secret, it would be discovered at the consummation of the marriage. How would this be done you may ask?

The husband would consummate the marriage (have sex with his wife) and then he would produce the bed sheet as evidence that his wife was a virgin. The blood that resulted from having sex with a virgin through the breakage of the hymen would be on the sheet and serve as evidence that she had kept herself pure.

If it was found out that she was not a virgin, the husband could take her to the elders of the community, who would pronounce her guilty and then she would be stoned to death. Unfair? Maybe, but that is how it was.

> *"Suppose a man marries a woman and, after sleeping with her, changes his mind about her [14] and falsely accuses her of having slept with another man. He might say, 'I discovered she was not a virgin when I married her.' [15] If the man does this, the woman's father and mother must bring the proof of her virginity to the leaders of the town.*
>
> *[16] Her father must tell them, 'I gave my daughter to this man to be his wife, and now he has turned against her. [17] He has accused her of shameful things, claiming that she was not a virgin when he married her. But here is the proof of my daughter's virginity.' Then they must spread the cloth before the judges.*

> *¹⁸ The judges must then punish the man. ¹⁹ They will fine him one hundred pieces of silver, for he falsely accused a virgin of Israel. The payment will be made to the woman's father. The woman will then remain the man's wife, and he may never divorce her. ²⁰ But suppose the man's accusations are true, and her virginity could not be proved.*
>
> *²¹ In such cases, the judges must take the girl to the door of her father's home, and the men of the town will stone her to death. She has committed a disgraceful crime in Israel by being promiscuous while living in her parents' home. Such evil must be cleansed from among you." (Deuteronomy 22:13-21)*

It is interesting to see how some guys have said they would like to marry a virgin yet they are doing everything to have sex with as many females as possible, including virgins. Where do they expect to find these virgins when they are ready to settle down?

Virginity tends to be viewed in a very negative way by some in our sex-crazed society. There is so much pressure placed upon those who are virgins. They are called weird and are told that there must be something wrong with them. Sometimes they are labeled as a homosexual or a lesbian just because they choose not to have sex.

This has caused some people who are virgins to lie about their sexual lives. They will say they are having sex, when they know they are not, just to avoid being the center of conversation or the brunt of jokes. This is very sad.

Many of the same people who are pressuring and making fun of those who are still virgins wish they could go back to being a virgin. What they thought or was told about having sex, was for them a disappointment or the person with whom they have had sex, is no longer in their lives. They are now angry and bitter, looking for others to join them.

In my talks to teens on this subject, I would often share a brief story about a girl that was being talked about, called names, and being made fun of just because she was a virgin.

One day she became tired of it and stood up to a group of girls who were making fun of her. She said the following:

"If I choose to, I could become like all of you any day, but you can never become like me ever again."

With that she walked away. That was the last she heard from them.

I would encourage these teens to do the same when they are being harassed over being a virgin. I would also add that they do so while they have a group of friends around for safety concerns.

CHAPTER SEVEN

Watch Out For the Bedroom!

9 But when she set the serving tray before him, he refused to eat. "Everyone get out of here," Amnon told his servants. So they all left.

10 Then he said to Tamar "Now bring the food into my bedroom and feed it to me here." So Tamar took it to him.

11 But as she was feeding him, he grabbed her and demanded, "Come to bed with me, my darling sister."

12 "No, my brother!" she cried. "Don't be foolish! Don't do this to me! You know what a serious crime it is to do such a thing in Israel.

13 Where could I go in my shame? And you would be called one of the greatest fools in Israel. Please, just speak to the king about it, and he will let you marry me."

14 But Amnon wouldn't listen to her, and since he was stronger than she was, he raped her

After everyone had left the room, Amnon responded to Tamar's earlier comment on the special meal request. "Oh, yeah. That is why I requested it. I know you are the best at making the stew. Hey, why don't you come in here when you are done and help me? I don't have the strength to get up from here."

"No problem. I understand. I'll be there as soon as I'm done. It won't take long," shouted Tamar from the kitchen.

"Okay," Amnon whispered as he began his Oscar-like performance.

Tamar completed the meal and then took it in to Amnon's room as he lay on his bed. She made herself comfortable, while he did the same. As she began to feed him, he held onto her hand as if to direct the food to his mouth. He continued to do so even when she moved the spoon away from his mouth.

Tamar, thinking that Amnon was playing around said laughingly, "What are you doing? I got it! You afraid I'm going to spill it, huh?"

She playfully tried to wrestle her hand away from Amnon, thinking that he too was being playful. She was very trusting of him.

As Tamar continued to pull her hand away, she winced as he tightened his grip. This felt very uncomfortable. Anxiety began to set in. Her eyes became moist as she began to fear the worst.

"I know you got it. That's not why I'm holding onto your hand. I want you to have sex with me. I love you. I know this is crazy, but I can't help it. I've been wanting this for a long time now."

Amnon by now had gotten up, moved the bowl out of the way and began to force her onto the bed.

"Let go of my hand", she said as firmly as she could while struggling to free hand. "You are hurting me. Are you *crazy*? You know this is wrong. This would be shameful. Don't! Let go of me!" She continued to try and wrestle her hand away from Amnon but to no avail.

When Tamar saw the look in his eyes and realized that he was very serious, she began to beg him not to. She told him to ask her dad - David, to let her marry him. (Marriage between family members was not uncommon in those days even though God did not approve it. It was culturally accepted as it is in some places today).

Even though she pleaded with him, he would not listen. She was unable to scream because he had his hand over her mouth. Even if he hadn't, she would not be able to get any words out because of the shock she was in. She was speechless and numb, all at the same time.

Being stronger than her, he forced her on the bed and raped her..

If raping her was not bad enough he told her to get out once he finished. She tried to reason with him but he wouldn't listen to her. He now felt hatred towards her and insisted that she leave. His feeling of hatred for her was stronger now than his previous feeling of love.

"You need to leave", Amnon said as he put his clothes on.

"Please Amnon, don't do that to me. Don't you have any feelings? Don't you care about me? Did you not just say a few minutes ago that you loved me? How can you now demand that I leave? I don't understand!"

Amnon raising his voice snapped at her, "Get out! What don't you understand? I never loved you. I want you to leave! Now!"

"No, sending me away would be worse than what you have already done", she said as she pleaded with him. Refusing to listen to her, he shouted for his servant to come and have her removed from the room. Realizing that he meant it, she hurriedly got dressed. She did her best not to look as distraught as she felt. She finished putting on her clothes just in time as the servant arrived.

"Get this woman out of here and away from me! Lock the door after her", he said to his servant.

While Amnon stood by the window looking outside, the servant took her by the hand, and forcefully removed her from the room. She was sobbing as she left but he - the servant, was unaware of the reason. He then bolted the door behind her.

Tamar was wearing a special robe with long sleeves, because the king's virgin daughters wore this kind of robe. To show how upset she was, she put ashes on her head (a sign of mourning), tore her special robe, and put her hand on her head. Then she went away, sobbing loudly.

Acquaintance Rape

Acquaintance rape is a sexual assault crime committed by someone whom the victim knows. It is also called date rape if the crime happens on a date. Being forced into having sex - even if it's by someone you know - is still rape and it's a crime.

Most sexual assaults are perpetrated by acquaintances of the victims, not strangers. According to a national study, 77 percent of rape survivors knew their attacker (2007 Study by the Miami University in Ohio).

Most acquaintance rapes happen to women ages 16 to 24.

Alcohol is a contributing factor to sexual assault. According to the same study, in 50 percent of all acquaintance rape cases on college campuses, both parties had been drinking; in 75 percent of cases, at least one party had been drinking. (2007 Study by the Miami University in Ohio)

Rape can never be justified under any circumstances. Unfortunately some have tried to justify rape and others have blamed the victim for such an act. Have you ever heard, when it comes to a female being raped by a male, that she "deserved it?" I've heard that.

To be honest with you I've had momentary thoughts when I see how little clothing and how seductively dressed some females are, that they (the females) are looking for trouble and if they got raped, they have no one to blame but themselves.

Thank God this is just a fleeting thought because I immediately appeal to my better senses that shouts out "no one is asking to be raped and rape cannot be justified!"

I know that rape is not just male against female. That used to be the most commonly reported kinds. However rape of boys by men and women, is now becoming more of a commonly reported crime. I would venture to say that there are more rapes happening but are not being reported.

My Story

My own experience went unreported, so I understand a little about the emotional dilemma facing boys in this position.

As a teen, I was almost raped by that trusted "friend" I spoke about in an earlier chapter. Even though it never actually happened, I still felt violated. It has been many years since the incident, and I still remember it as if it were yesterday. I never told anyone or talked about it for many, many years.

I was ashamed.

I was in denial.

I felt stupid for not being smarter and for being so trusting.

I did see the perpetrator after the incident and even talked with him but slowly withdrew myself.

This may be the typical response of male victims who do not report such crimes, which may account for the underreporting of sexual assaults on males. The U.S. Bureau of Justice Statistics (1999) estimated that 91% of U.S. rape victims are female and 9% are male.

As one who has had a close call with all the feelings evoked by that incident, I could not imagine what it must be like for someone who has actually been raped. I do know that some of the feelings that I experienced are similar but are more intense for the victims of such crime.

Guilt, shame, anger plus a whole host of emotions fills the hearts of victims. So many victims are suffering in silence. Some are doing so not only because of shame or guilt, but also from fear. Most times perpetrators use threats as a way of silencing the victim. These threats could be against the family or the victim.

Victims may not know where to go, whom to trust, or who would believe them. Some have told other family members - maybe a parent, but was told that they should not say anything to anyone about it and in some cases it would be taken care of but usually never does.

This is especially true when it involves a family member. The US Department of Justice, based on a study in 1991 of 11 states, found that 96 percent of the female rape victims, who were younger than 12 years old, knew their attackers, and twenty percent were victimized by their fathers.

In a study done by Abbey, A., BeShears, R., Clinton-Sherrod, A. M., & McAuslan, P. (2004) and reported in Psychology of Women Quarterly, strangers victimized only two percent of female rape victims. That means that ninety-eight percent were by acquaintances or family members.

I have spoken to and counseled female clients who have shared their experience of being sexually molested by a step-dad or a mother's lover. One of the recurring complaints I hear from these clients is that when they told their moms about what had happened, they were not believed.

One of my clients even told me that they were accused of making up the story and then being called a lying b***h.

Others have been told that it was their fault and are blamed for what has happened. Still some are protecting the perpetrator for one reason or another.

Maybe self-blame is one of the strongest reasons for some not to come forward.

If you happen to be a victim, let me say as strongly as I can - GET HELP IMMEDIATELY! Remember it is not your fault! You were taken advantage of. Guilt says "I did something wrong". What did *you* do wrong? Someone else did you wrong. They should be the one carrying the guilt. Not you! You need to talk to someone who you can trust. This needs to be brought to the forefront. Imagine another person somewhere out there - a younger child or family member, being subjected to a similar fate. You have information to possibly stop that. If you think you are protecting someone, you really aren't. You are protecting someone who never thought about protecting you.

When Amnon invited Tamar to come into his room to serve him the food, "red flags" should be going up at this point. "Alarm bells" should have been going off in Tamar's head. Unfortunately most young people and even some adults, will see these "red flags" or hear these "bells" yet totally ignore them. This might be because of their innocence or naïveté.

Could this have been Tamar's downfall?

The following advice is applicable when you have knowledge or suspicion regarding the intent of another person. Both Tamar and myself were caught off guard. It was the last thing on our minds.

Having said that, as a female, you want to avoid being by yourself with someone who you suspect or know has his or her "eyes" on you; that is, he or she is showing interest in you. This is also true for guys. We have witnessed a surge in female on male as well as same-sex sexual assaults, that it is imperative to impress this admonition on the males as well.

Two of those places to be avoided when you are by yourselves, are in a room or a parked car on a dimly lit street,.

Avoid being alone with him or her as much as possible. Being on the offense is one of your best defenses. You can do this by telling him or her what you will not do or tolerate and are expecting them to respect your wishes.

There are no guarantees such precautionary measures will prevent sexual assaults, but it could lead to the minimization of the attempts. Be vigilant in reminding the other person who maybe suffering from short-term memory, what your boundaries and values are. Do it quickly.

One of the many sayings I heard growing up, is, "if you give a person an inch, he or she will take a mile." Don't give them an inch. This applies so much more to the Devil.

What Amnon was about to do to her was the last thing on her mind. Maybe this is why she so willingly took the food to his room. She could never have imagined that what happened to her, would come at the hands of one she thought she knew well.

It is easier to be taken advantage of by someone who looks, acts and sounds trustworthy, than it is by someone who projects an opposite demeanor.

We do not want to go around profiling people and making a conclusion based upon the external only. Should the external be used? Sure, but not exclusively. How would you like someone to not trust you based solely on the fact of how you look?

With that said, we must use wisdom. It is always good to operate from a position of caution. Do not go into relationship, (business or friendship), or accept offers without doing some kind of investigation. At the same time give yourself enough time to make an informative decision. Do not rush into any relationship

It's naive to think that someone is not capable of doing the most despicable things possible. In the book of Jeremiah chapter 17:9, we find this caution about our heart: "The heart is deceitful above all things, and desperately wicked; who can know it?" Our heart is capable of just about anything one can think of or imagine. Do not put anything past the human heart.

I'm sure you have done things that you thought you would never have done. I know that I have. Most people I know, when asked if they have done things they thought they would never have done, have said yes. I love what Max Lucado says, "let your failures refine you, not define you."

Even though this thought was stated earlier, I believe it is worth repeating. When you are with someone to whom you are attracted it is an advisable thing to never be with him or her alone with no one else around. This could be at home when no one else is there or in a parked car in a remote or dimly lit place.

This also applies if you have an indication or inclination that the other person is attracted to you. It is really important that you know this. It should be something you avoid, if at all possible. I know there are times because of work or school activities, you cannot avoid such contact. However, be cautious.

No one can blame Tamar for doing what she thought was a very safe and innocent act. Who would have ever thought she would experience what happened to her.

This was not supposed to happen.

So many people including myself, share such a thought. Maybe you are sharing this thought as well. If so, get some help. Talk to someone as soon as possible.

Here are some suggestions as to possible people that you could talk with regarding your situation: Your Priest, Rabbi, Pastor, Spiritual Leader, or Professional Counselor.

Get help today!

CHAPTER EIGHT

As A Result Of Sexual Trauma

***20** Her brother Absalom saw her and asked, "Is it true that Amnon has been with you? Well, don't be so upset. Since he's your brother anyway, don't worry about it." So Tamar lived as a desolate woman in Absalom's house. **21** When King David heard what had happened, he was very angry. **22** And though Absalom never spoke to Amnon about it, he hated Amnon deeply because of what he had done to his sister*

Tamar was in great pain physically, mentally, and emotionally. It was very evident in her walk as she made her way towards her house.

As she did, she encountered her brother, Absalom.

"What's wrong little sis? What's the matter? Why are you looking so sad? Why the torn garbs?" Absalom knew the meaning of a torn garb. It meant one thing ... violated. He slowly said, *"Don't tell me Amnon forced himself on you. I know dad had sent you to see him"*

Tamar just continued to sob as he held her in his arms. She shook her head confirming his fears. Tears were welling up in his eyes but she could not see them as she had her head buried in his chest.

When Absalom confirmed with Tamar what his suspicion was, he not only tried to comfort her through his hugs, but also by his words. However, his good intentions were partially ill conceived. I will explain that in a few moments.

"For now baby, don't say anything to anyone. Keep this to yourself. He is your half-brother. Don't let this upset you so much! C'mon let me take you home."

So Tamar went with him and stayed at his house. She realized she now had a "secret" she could not share with anyone. It became a family secret.

She started to feel depressed as she crawled into the bed. As she lay there her mind began to wander.

One of the first things that came to her mind was the conversation with her brother Absalom. She began to think of what he just said to her, "Don't let this upset you so much!"

"What do you mean 'don't let this upset me so much?'", she thought to herself.

"Are you saying that I should not worry *much* about it." Really? What should I *not* be worried about? The shame? The possibility of pregnancy? The possibility of an acquired STD? My future? Which one?" She could feel her anger rising the more she thought about it.

"Are *you* kidding, Absalom? Don't worry!"

Good Intention, Bad Timing

Absalom's words to Tamar, "don't let this upset you so much" are ones that are repeated over and over again.

Even though Absalom intended well and had Tamar's best interest at heart, he was basically minimizing or ignoring her feelings. However, good intentions does not make certain statements or actions right. We need to be careful of what we say to others especially when they are in pain or going through a difficult time.

It is so easy to tell someone not to feel what he or she is feeling.

This is one of the main issues that I highlight in sessions on communication. Some of the complaints I have by a family member or a spouse especially a wife is that their feelings are being ignored.

One of my favorite sayings is that "feelings are neither right or wrong. They just are. It is what you do with the feelings that matter." I then emphasize that it is the behavior stemming from the feelings that is either right or wrong.

Here's what *not* to do when someone has experienced something that they consider to be a painful experience.

Don't do what Absalom did ...

Don't tell that person that you understand what they are going through because you really don't.

Don't tell them how to feel.

The best thing we can do for that person is to pray for them and trust God to heal them. In the meantime, be a good listener.

One of the many things I do know about God and that is, he's able and willing to heal the hurt and pain being experienced. He is willing to grant his grace, mercy, and strength to those who seek it.

The Effects of Sexual Trauma

Not only was Tamar wrestling with the thought of what her brother Absalom said to her, she now began to think of the possibility of pregnancy.

"What if I became pregnant?" she thought to herself. "What will I do?"

"Do I have an abortion?"

"Do I give the child up for an adoption?"

"Will Amnon want to keep the baby?"

These are just some of the questions running through her mind as she lay on the bed.

One of the most contested and prolonged debates surrounding pregnancy has to do with the issue of abortion. Some women, who become pregnant after a rape, may feel abortion is their only choice. Through an abortion, a child is punished for something they had nothing to do with. The emotional and mental toll of taking the life of an innocent child may not be immediately felt. It will be felt at a later date.

I can hear the arguments that keeping the child will only serve as a constant reminder to such a horrific crime.

Who would argue against that?

Here's my first reaction to that argument. Would anyone ever forget such an act?

What about other factors such as certain scents (perfume or Cologne) or places such as a hotel, park, house, being touched a certain way, sounds, etc? These will stimulate the senses: visual (sense of seeing), auditory (sense of hearing), olfactory (sense of smell) and the kinesthetic (sense of touch). They all will serve as reminders. What does a victim do about these?

No matter what the reason, abortion is still about the taking of a life. God clearly says we are fearfully and wonderfully made. This he declares at conception. (Psalm 139:13-16)

Millions of babies have died as a result of abortion. Many women have signed on to abortion because they are not well informed. Some have done it out of economic, social, and other personal conveniences. Still others have done so out of disregard for the sanctity of life.

Abortion has many consequences, most of which is not being reported. As a counselor, I have counseled individuals who have had abortions, and years later, still are reliving the nightmares. They now have to deal with the emotional and mental consequences. Most of this is not being reported and probably will not, because of the political and financial implications.

The notion that a woman has a right to her body and should be able to do with it whatever she wants, clouds the issue. What about the right of the unborn? Mary, mother of Jesus, knew the gender of her child at conception. She was told that she was going to have a male child even before she knew she was pregnant. She also knew what his name was going to be called, Jesus. The implication is that her son was not a blob of tissue, but indeed a human being who had a gender and a name even before conception.

Just in case one would argue that this is just a single incident, we could look back before Jesus' birth to Jeremiah who became one of Israel's most effective prophets and also an incredible leader.

He and God had a conversation, in which God told him that he knew him before he was born, and had assigned him with the task of being a spokesperson for him. Here is how it reads, Jeremiah 1:5, "I knew you before I formed you in your mother's womb. Before you were born I set you apart and appointed you as my spokesman to the world."

Another significant passage of scripture is found in Psalm 139, where the passage gives clear evidence that God is the one that forms us in a very intricate way:

[13] You made all the delicate, inner parts of my body and knit me together in my mother's womb.
[14] Thank you for making me so wonderfully complex! Your workmanship is marvelous—and how well I know it.

[15] You watched me as I was being formed in utter seclusion, as I was woven together in the dark of the womb.

[16] You saw me before I was born. Every day of my life was recorded in your book. Every moment was laid out before a single day had passed. (Psalm 139:13-16)

This is a vivid description of how complex the human body is, and God's involvement in the process. This also rebuffs the claims of evolution. The question is this: "if it is not the taking of life, then what *is* it?"

The alternatives to abortion are adoption or keeping the baby. Adoption is a gift of love to a family who desires to have a child but not being able to do so for medical or other reasons. It is an option that fills a void in so many people's lives. There are many loving arms that await a child who would otherwise be aborted, abused, or neglected. This is a great alternative.

Much has been written and debated over the years on the above subject matter. I have no doubt such debates will continue. It's not my intention to use this book for such purposes. However, I wanted to add my voice to this topic of which I'm passionate about.

Getting Married Just Because

One of the decisions that so many couples have made is to get married because of a pregnancy. This often turns out to be a mistake.

Even though each person is responsible to make their own decision, I will almost always try to have them delay the process so that they can take time to consider all their options. Not only that, but if they wait, the chance is they will allow their emotions to be normalized, which may or may not lead to marriage. At least, not at this point anyway.

I have seen and read of a number of couples that got married just because a pregnancy occurred. To "cover" it up and to appease the parents, they make the decision to get married.

What those who chose marriage, as a "cover-up" need to realize is that there is no "covering-up." The truth will come out one day. As long as someone else knows about this, it is no longer a secret. Secondly, it is not hard to do the math.

I know in Tamar's situation, the thought of marriage would not be one of the options that she would be entertaining at this point. She did suggest that to

Amnon at first but obviously that was not on his mind. He just wanted the sex and nothing more.

That is how some guys approach relationships. My counsel to females is that they should avoid sexual intercourse until marriage, and build the relationship around communication, conflict resolution, spirituality, and other social skills. This is a good way to see what the ulterior motives are. Even though this is not a guarantee, it is one way to get to know more about that individual.

Unfortunately, Tamar, as well as so many others, did not have that opportunity.

At this point Tamar needed support. She needed someone to just be there for her. She was feeling so alone. She was in a daze.

Whenever you are in your darkest moment, God always finds a way to attend to us. We find that happening throughout the Bible. He will send help our way. The important thing is that we have to be open, sensitive, and receptive to such. We could easily miss those opportunities.

I heard a story (which has no scriptural basis but it makes the point) of a flood that kept on rising from days of rain. One of the members of the community happened to be a pastor whose house was almost covered with water. He climbed onto the roof of the house waiting to be rescued. The first rescuers arrived in a boat and extended to him a ladder. He refused to come down because he said that God was going to rescue him. The rescuers pleaded with him to come down, but to no avail. They had no choice but to leave.

Eventually a helicopter hovered over his house and dropped a device for him to climb into so they could take him to safety. Again he refused, telling them that God was going to rescue him. They also pleaded with him, but to no avail. They had no other choice but to leave.

The water rose and he could no longer go any higher so he was swept away to his death.

He showed up in heaven and the first question was to ask God why he did not rescue him.

God said, "I tried to rescue you on two occasions but you refused. What more did you want me to do?"

The man realized that God had indeed made an attempt, but *he* was not receptive to the choice of rescue that God had sent.

We need to be careful not to turn away God's choice of rescue when we are in a difficult situation.

Pain can cause us not to hear, see, or think clearly. These are the times we could be most vulnerable to be taken advantage of. It could also cause us to shut everyone and everything out.

Issues Surrounding Rape

One of the thoughts that Tamar may also be processing, is how will she respond sexually in the future to someone with whom she falls in love and possibly end up marrying.

Sexual trauma can have an adverse effect upon individuals within a marriage. Men can suffer from some form of erectile dysfunction while women could possibly suffer from dyspareunia (painful intercourse) or vaginismus (an involuntary spasm of the muscles of the vaginal wall, which interferes with intercourse). Most of these are anxiety related dysfunctions.

These are just a few of the sexual issues that individuals could possibly face as a result of a trauma such as rape.

If she developed a relationship and began to court for marriage, she has to wrestle with the thought of whether or not she should tell her fiancé about her past, and if so, when. Does she tell him while they are courting for marriage, after marriage, or does she keep it to herself? What would you do?

If and when Tamar got married, she might have nightmares whenever she and her husband become intimate. It might become hard for her to separate these two acts.

Unfortunately Tamar did not live in this century. If she did, I would have strongly recommended that she get professional help to sort through some of these issues. Due to confidentiality issues I would recommend she does this on an individual basis prior to marriage.

The exception to this is if she is planning to get married and decides to do pre-marital counseling. These issues would then need to be discussed.

As a Marriage and Family Counselor, I would definitely recommend that she does joint sessions so that her husband would not only get a better understanding of what sexual trauma does to someone, but also find ways to help her work through these issues. His support and understanding are paramount to her recovery. This is no longer her issue but *their* issue because of the affect it is having on the relationship.

This therapeutic work requires a very dedicated, patient and loving husband who is very committed to the relationship and the process.

It would be to Tamar's advantage to choose such a person.

This will require that she spend a considerable amount of time with her potential husband to see how patient he is with *his* family and friends. She cannot ignore or try to explain away any indication that he does not have this very important quality. She is going to need it. She also should not get married without doing pre-marital counseling. There is too much at stake.

My professional recommendation to her would be to date for at least twelve to eighteen months, then enter a four to six months premarital counseling arrangement.

Even though Tamar may be wrestling with the above-mentioned issues, it is also true that she on the other hand, could become sexually promiscuous.

So many females have resorted to this lifestyle, at least temporarily, as a way of dealing with their pain. They may no longer feel pretty. Their self-esteem has been lowered significantly. The one thing that was meaningful to them has been taken away. This may lead them into a downward spiral of alcoholism, cutting, drugs, and promiscuity - just a few of the psychological problems that come as a result of a rape. These become a form of self-medication in trying to numb or reduce the pain. This is also true of some men as well but it is more prevalent among the female population.

Other issues such as sexual identity could possibly emerge. A person who was sexually molested by someone of the same gender, may associate sex acts as some thing to be experienced with same-sex partners. This is especially true if it took place at an early age. This could create some confusion for them.

Someone who may have consented to the act, but was not of age, or who was taking advantage of by a person who was an authority or had a celebratory status, could also have some confusion around sexual identity. This is much more so if they took pleasure in the act.

When small children experience sexual assault, there is a tendency to act-out in sexual ways with other children and sometimes with older individuals. Some of these ways may be exposing themselves to their peers, having their genitals being touched or touching other children's genitals or any other form of inappropriate sexual behavior. If this does happen, that child needs to get professional help immediately. This becomes a "red flag" for further investigation or exploration.

There are so much more that could be said about the issues surrounding sexual trauma that as I have done throughout this book, recommend strongly that victims seek professional help.

CHAPTER NINE

When The Dust Settles

As Tamar lay on the bed, she pulled her knees as close as she could to her chest. She is curled up with one pillow under her head and the other clutched tightly to her chest along with her small, soft, beige, fluffy Teddy Bear.

Her emotions are all over the place. She is in shock. She is in pain. She is numb and in disbelief. She is hoping this really did not happen, but was a nightmare and that she would wake up from this really bad dream.

She is sobbing. Here are questions you need to honestly ask yourself as you ponder if you are being loved:

How is this person seeking to *protect* me and *provide* for me? Her eyes, puffed from crying. Her mouth is dry. She closes and opens her eyes trying to focus but somehow having a very difficult time doing so. She is replaying what Amnon had done to her. She was going through all the frames of the event looking to see if or how it could have been avoided. Each frame of the evening is looked at almost microscopically - frame by frame. She rewinds the "tape" over and over again, pausing here and there, trying to see what she had missed.

She was looking to see if she had missed a clue that would have alerted her to what took place. Did she overlook something? Was she too trusting?

Even though she was the victim, the burden of proof rested on her. If she did not scream or cry for help, then it could be argued that she consented. Amnon could make this case. She knew that.

She was able to come up with two clues. The *first* was Amnon asking his servants and the others to leave his room. She remembered how strange that request sounded to her.

"Why would he ask them to leave," she thought.

The *second* clue was Amnon asking her to come into the bedroom and serve him the meal. This request was even stranger. "Why would he want me to come into his room and serve him," she thought to herself. "I guess he must really be sick."

These were not enough clues for her to be overly suspicious to the point of leaving or making sure someone else was in the room with them.

Most times, it is the person we least suspect who ends up doing the evil deed.

How many times have we heard stories on the news of someone appealing to the public for their help to solve a lingering case? A mom appealing for help to find her child; a husband appealing for help to find the person or persons responsible for his wife's death; a wife appealing for help in a similar situation; a neighbor helping to look for or hand out fliers for a missing neighbor or a suspect.

These stories tug at our hearts until we find out that the person making the appeal or helping in the search, is the one guilty of the crime. It is the person we least suspected.

So it was with Tamar. The person she least suspected - Amnon, was the one who ended up raping her.

She now began to think of what could she have done differently. This question is one of blaming self. All the what-ifs are now racing through her mind.

"What if I had screamed!"

"What if I hadn't gone to his house?"

"What if Dad had been smart enough to say no to Amnon's request?"

"What if I had insisted that the servants stay inside the house?"

What if! What if! What if!

Have you ever been there? Have you ever had to say "what if?"

Not only was she asking the "what if" questions, but she began to ask "why."

Why me?

Why was I so stupid?

Why God, why!

Why dad, why?

Why Amnon, why?

I can almost hear her asking "why me" over and over again in between each sob. She is screaming into her pillow as loudly as she can, hoping the sound is muffled, so no one can hear her.

Why?

Have you ever asked that question? I know I have. Many times. Even though this is a three-letter word, it is one of the biggest and longest words when we are in pain.

I asked why, after years of suppression of my experience of almost being raped by someone that I considered to be a friend. A friend? Well, let's say, an acquaintance.

The more I have thought about that word - why, the more I wonder what difference would it make even if I was told. Would it change anything? Would it make it more understandable? Would it make it better? Would the pain be any less? Would my offender be able to give me back what he took from me?

He incurred a debt he cannot pay.

Even though we know that our offender cannot pay us back, we still ask why.

Jesus, while on the cross, asked "why." He did so, not because he did not know the reason, but because of what he was feeling and experiencing at the time. His pain was unparalleled from any other human encounter.

His "why" was not a demanding why as if Father God owed him an explanation. It was one of submission that his Father was in control and had his best interest at heart.

Sometime asking why is used as a means of relieving the pent up stress that one feels.

In the book of Matthew chapter 27:46 (NLT), the scripture says that at about three o'clock, Jesus called out with a loud voice, "Eli, Eli, lema sabachthani?" which means, "My God, my God, why have you forsaken me?"

He felt lonely, forsaken and maybe even abandoned — left all alone to suffer and die. He felt what it was like to be out of the presence of his Father for that moment. He experienced, temporarily, what we will one day experience permanently, should we refuse to accept his invitation to live with him for eternity.

He is also able to empathize with our "why." He has been there. He has gone through it. All the feelings we will ever have when it comes to trauma or emotional and physical pain, he experienced. Why? So that when we come to him, he can comfort us. With that comfort we can comfort others as Paul states in 2 Corinthians 1:4, *"He comforts us in all our troubles so that we can comfort others. When others are troubled, we will be able to give them the same comfort God has given us."*

No one knows what it feels like to go through a particular pain, like one who has been through it themselves. A person of experience tends to be more credible than one who does not have such. It makes them more authentic, at least on the surface.

The Bible says, "the veil was torn in two" – Mark 15:38. This was symbolic of an entrance being opened allowing access. The access that was granted was for all of us who would one day ask why. Inside that room sits one who understands and is awaiting us to come with our "whys".

In Matthew 11:28 Jesus made this very important statement, "Come to me, all of you who are weary and carry heavy burdens *[your whys]*, and I will give you rest." [italics mine]

That is a promise that He stands by. He feels our pain and wants to offer us the comfort we need. No one else is able to do that for us. No amount of "sorry" is going to help. It is a necessary step, but the ultimate help and release comes from Jesus. Our pain touches his heart. He's been there. He stands ready to help us.

This would have been my advice for Tamar if I was there or if she had sought out my help – bring it to Jesus.

Trauma and depression

As the days passed, Tamar began to feel depressed. She does not want to get up. She has no strength, no appetite and wishes she could close her eyes and never open them again. She felt like dying. Have you ever felt that way?

The stigma, shame, and possible isolation, added to her stress. She knew the consequences of not being a virgin prior to marriage. She began to show some of the symptoms that would qualify her as clinically depressed. Depression is one of the most common mood disorders of sexual trauma.

There are huge numbers of resources available, both in print and electronically, on the topic of depression. I will not bore you with all the statistics, or with a neurological or physiological explanation of depression.

According to the popular website www.webmd.com, *"feeling depressed is a normal reaction to loss, life's struggles, or an injured self-esteem. But when these feelings become overwhelming and last for long periods of time, they can keep you from leading a normal, active life. That's when it's time to seek medical help.*

If left untreated, symptoms of clinical or major depression may worsen and last for years. They can cause untold suffering and possibly lead to suicide. Recognizing the symptoms of depression is often the biggest hurdle to the diagnosis and treatment of clinical or major depression.

Unfortunately, approximately half the people who experience symptoms never do get diagnosed or treated for their illness. Not getting treatment can be life threatening. More than one out of every 10 people battling depression commits suicide." (*"Signs of Clinical Depression: Symptoms to Watch For,"* 1999)

What are symptoms of depression?

According to the National Institute of Mental Health, symptoms of depression may include the following:

- Difficulty concentrating, remembering details, and making decisions
- Fatigue and decreased energy
- Feelings of guilt, worthlessness, and/or helplessness
- Feelings of hopelessness and/or pessimism
- Insomnia, early-morning wakefulness, or excessive sleeping
- Irritability, restlessness
- Loss of interest in activities or hobbies once pleasurable, including sex
- Overeating or appetite loss
- Persistent aches or pains, headaches, cramps, or digestive problems that do not ease even with treatment
- Persistent sad, anxious, or "empty" feelings
- Thoughts of suicide, suicide attempts

("Signs of Clinical Depression: Symptoms to Watch For," 1999)

If someone is experiencing five or more of these symptoms for a period of two weeks or more, they should seek professional help as soon as possible. Let me hasten to say that this list should not be used to diagnose yourself or someone else. Leave such a diagnosis to a licensed mental health professional.

Depression carries a high risk of suicide. Anybody who expresses suicidal thoughts or intentions should be taken very, very seriously. Do not hesitate to call your local suicide hotline immediately.

Trauma and Suicide

Even though I cannot recall thinking about suicide, I know of many who have and of others who have actually committed suicide. The pain of sexual traumas can become very excruciating. Suicide seems like an attractable alternative. Tamar may have considered suicide as a viable option. She may have weighed this option and decided against it.

So many people today are choosing this path, especially teenagers. Suicide is the third leading cause of death among teenagers today. It is steadily rising as more and more teens are experiencing bullying, stereotyping, and low self-esteem issues - just to name a few leading causes of suicide.

Most people at some point in their lives have entertained thoughts of suicide. Having a thought periodically does not mean that you are necessarily suicidal. What makes one suicidal is the prevailing thought of killing themselves and most importantly, planning how they would accomplish it.

As a therapist, whenever I assess for suicidal thoughts, I ask my clients how they plan to commit the act. I ask for specifics such as date, time, place, and method.

One of the interventions used, is a suicide contract where I will ask the client to do certain things if or when they feel like committing the act. One of those action plans is to make a phone call. I will also outline a task that they will have to do and report at the next session. This creates an accountability component.

In extreme cases, the client may have to be baker-acted. Baker-acting is a process by which a client is committed to a mental health institute for seventy-two hours to be assessed. This also gives them time to "cool off."

Suicide is never a solution. It is self-serving and only adds one more layer of complication for the family left behind. It is permanent and is Satan's lie. Do not believe him! Having said that, it is understandable why someone would entertain suicidal thoughts but it's not the only option.

Case And Point

September 22, 2010

Just before the writing of this chapter, there was an incident at Rutgers University in New Jersey, which led to the suicide of 18-year old Tyler Clementi.

Reports of events leading to his death state that his male roommate and another female friend had videotaped him having sex with another male companion. The "friends" uploaded the video to the Internet and sent out an electronic message, describing the post.

Tyler found out about the broadcast of his sexual encounter. He had not "come out" to his parents about being homosexual. Now, in his mind, the "whole world" knew. This was too unbearable for him. He went to the George Washington Bridge and jumped to his death. His roommate and the other student were charged with invasion of privacy. Other charges are also pending.

Tamar could have resorted to this method as so many do. I would dare say you may have had previous thoughts of suicide or know some one who has. You may be having such thoughts right now.

If you are having suicidal ideations (thoughts), let me remind you that suicide is permanent and it *never* solves the problem. I strongly suggest that you get help immediately. There are people who care about you and want what is best for you. It may not be your parents or a family member, even though they should be the first line of help. It could be your minister, priest, rabbi, teacher, friend, mentor, or counselor - any trusted adult.

As I stated before, having a suicidal thought that is not lasting, does not necessarily mean that you are suicidal or have suicidal tendencies. Almost everyone has had such a thought at one point or another. Having the thought is not the issue. It is the frequency and duration of the reoccurrences that is concerning.

If you are experiencing a pattern of reoccurring thoughts as outlined above, please get professional help immediately.

Most countries have a system in place that caters to individuals who are having suicidal ideations. Check with your local, city, or state office for such information.

If you are in the United States of America you can dial 1-800-SUICIDE (1-800-784-2433) or 1-800-273-TALK (1-800-273-8255).

Anyone who has gone through similar trauma can identify with Tamar. You might be feeling her pain as you read this. Old wounds of yours might be re-opened. You might be having a hard time with this as you relive your own pain.

If that is true of you I would strongly suggest you get some help as quickly as possible. Talk with someone as suggested earlier.

This was not supposed to happen to *me*

It was the person I least suspected that almost raped me.

As I recall my own situation and what could have happened, my thoughts continuously expand. I ponder these questions:

Who would have believed me?

What would they have thought about me?

Would they think I'm gay?

This was very humiliating. As an athletic and popular guy, the last thing that I would want to happen is for my friends thinking negative thoughts of me. I could hear the jokes and the side remarks. I can just imagine walking into a room and have the conversation stop. Every small group that looked my way as I pass by or approach them would only confirm my suspicion ... *they* are talking about me.

Like me, so many who have had a close call or been actually molested, have chosen to keep it a secret. I am an advocate for letting someone know because that person could do it to someone else. They have to be stopped.

Having said that, I know the difficulty of doing so. I did not because of shame. I felt humiliated. I would rather live with the pain for the rest of my life.

I have heard from and spoken with victims, who would rather take the position I took than tell someone about it. One of the reasons that I hear over and over again, surrounds blame. They blame themselves for putting themselves in that situation, for

So many like me would rather suffer-in-silence,

allowing repeated occurrences or for allowing it to go on for so long and not doing anything at the time.

There are those on the other hand who have attempted to tell someone but wish they had not because of what they were told.

"It's your fault"

"If you were not wearing the clothes you were, that would not have happened!"

"If you had listened to me, then that might not have happened".

"Don't tell anyone about this. We will take care of it," *(but they generally never do).*

"You are lying!"

These are just some of what these victims experienced. Others have read about comments like these and have decided not to take the risk.

Some statistics have shown where one out of four boys and one out of three girls have been victims of sexual assault and this is only based on those who have reported such crime. I would have been one of those who never did.

As hard as it is, I would strongly urge anyone who has been victimized, to tell someone. There is someone out there who will believe you. There are those like myself who are out there. Look around. Make it your goal to get it out. I wished I had done that. I wished I grew up in a more embracing culture that was not as judgmental as it was, having such so-called high standards where people like me would feel more comfortable in talking about such experience.

Did I Not See It Coming?

As I have reflected upon what could have possibly happened to me, I have wrestled with this thought: "Did I not see it coming!"

In reading the story of Tamar, I have also thought about that. Were there any signs as to what Amnon was planning for her?

When you are not expecting something bad to happen, you will overlook signs that, in hindsight, blared at you. It is hard to know if Tamar or her dad had any suspicion of Amnon. There is no indication that they did.

As I pondered my situation, I began to look at all the pieces. This guy had invited me to spend the night at his home instead of making the long trek to my home, which would be quite difficult for me at that time of night. How thoughtful! Suspicious? No need to suspect here.

I did not know him well. He was a customer who would come to the bank where I worked. One thing I do know is that he had a very good job and as far as I know, was well respected at his job. We developed a teller-customer relationship. He became an acquaintance of mine.

> Most times, it is the person we suspect the least who ends up doing the evil deed.

Suspicious? Maybe.

Why?

I did not know him well, but to my defense, I was young, it was late, and I had no way home.

Prior to this, I did not know of anyone who was either a homosexual or have homosexual tendencies. If there were people who had such tendencies, they would not have made it public. I would imagine there were a number of people who chose to stay in the "closet" rather than face the consequences of "coming out." I personally do not remember anyone who was "out."

This was another reason why such a thought would be the farthest from my mind.

Having gotten to his house, there was nothing said at the time or done that would raise my suspicion. I was like a lamb going to the slaughter.

The only thing that I could have been suspicious of, was his response to my statement of not having clothes in which to sleep. He said, *"I should not worry about it. I could just sleep in my underwear"*

I thought that I would be sleeping on the couch because he only had a one-bedroom townhouse. However, he insisted that he could not have his guest sleep on the couch so I should share the bed with him. He had a queen or king size bed. I cannot recall the size. I only knew it was a large bed.

Whenever I have slept in a bed with another male, I have made it a practice to turn my back to them and make sure we do not touch during the night. If possible, I try to make sure we have separate sheets covering us. I have done this on many mission trips as well as other occasions, such as men's retreats, etc.

Being a naive and trusting teenager (I was almost 19 years old at this time), I went along with the suggestion.

I thought that it was rather nice of him to offer me a space on his bed to sleep.

At some point during the night, I felt him getting closer to me. Again, my back was turned towards him, which I now know was not a good idea. He was close enough that I felt his body next to mine. I was aware of him then. I knew, this was *not* a dream.

In a sheepish way, I gradually moved away from him. I did not want to make it obvious. I pretended that I was shifting in my sleep and moved an inch or two at a time, away from him.

I could only do this for so long without making it obvious, and I was running out of space on the bed. At this point I just laid there in a state of shock as I felt him pulling down my underwear.

At this point I could pretend no more. It was getting serious and definitely too close for comfort. I had no idea what time it was, but I was determined to get out of the bed and if needed, get dressed and leave.

Not wanting to embarrass him or let him on to the fact that I knew what was happening. I got up and went to the bathroom. As I got out of the bed I noticed that there was a jar of Vaseline on the nightstand on his side of the bed. I did not notice it there before going to bed.

I stayed in the bathroom for what seemed like eternity hoping dawn would come quickly, while pondering what my next move will be.

"How do I leave?"

"What do I say to him?"

"Do I go back into the bed?"

These were just some of the questions and thoughts I was having while in the bathroom.

I eventually went back into the bed, I lay on my back with my eyes closed but moving every minute or so. I'm not sure if he knew that I was now aware of what he was trying to do, because he did not attempt to try anything again. I also noticed, before I lay down that the Vaseline was no longer on the stand.

> *I have since come to understand it was not my fault and I had nothing to be ashamed about*

I laid there for what seemed like an eternity, and then decided to get up and get dressed. I was going to leave and try to get a cab to my house. I had to go there anyway so that I could get dressed for work.

It was now about 4:30 a.m. People who had to go to work via public transportation would have been up and the cabs and buses would now be on the road. I got dressed, thanked him for allowing me to stay and then left.

I went out the door as quickly as I could, feeling very relieved but also in a state of shock. I knew right away that I would never tell anyone about this. No one could find out. Our culture was very anti-homosexual. If I told someone, would I be labeled a homosexual? I was not ready to find out so I kept it to myself for almost 20 years.

I have since come to understand it was not my fault and I had nothing to be ashamed about. I did not ask for this to happen to me, and I pray that, by sharing my story, it might help others who might find themselves in my situation.

Other than her brother Absalom, we do not know if Tamar spoke with anyone else about the rape.

CHAPTER TEN

Put The Lid On Anger!

Anger is one of the strongest emotions experienced as a result of sexual violation. Alongside the emotion of anger is fear. These two emotions are often experienced simultaneously. Anger is centered on what happened in the past, while fear is centered on how what happened, will affect us in the future.

Anger is a God-given emotion that is a normal part of life. Healthy anger has tremendous potential for good. Anger only becomes a problem when we deny, suppress, repress, stuff and ignore it or when we don't listen to it, understand it and allow it to serve its God-intended function. (Caring for People God's Way 2005, pp 213)

In Ephesian 4:26, we are given permission to express the emotion of anger. The Bible says, "Be angry …". That is the permission part of the verse. However the verse did not end there. It follows up immediately with "… and sin not". This is the cautionary or warning side of the verse. As much as we should express the emotion of anger, we are told to not allow it to cause us to sin. The sin is the behavior that follows. Whatever is done out of anger, is sin.

The more Tamar thought about what Amnon did to her the angrier she became. A part of her wanted justice. She was experiencing an "injustice gap" – the difference between the way she would like what Amnon did to her to be resolved and the way it seems to be going right now. He seemed to be getting away with it. He is not experiencing any negative effects of what he did. He got what he wanted and life seems to be going on – life as usual. This was not the case for her.

Tamar's fear is on her future. Whenever she begins to think about what she will *not* be able to experience because of the rape, she becomes even angrier.

Her anger could also be directed at God as is the case for so many people who have experienced a horrible trauma. The anger is based upon the fact that God who is Omnipotent (all-powerful), Omniscient (all-knowing), and Omnipresent (everywhere present), would seemingly sit by idle and allow this to happen. The thought is that God must not be caring as she thought or he must not be as powerful. If he were, then why did he not do some thing.

I have met people and worked with some in counseling sessions that do not want to hear the name of God during the session. They are very turned off from him. They are having a hard time reconciling what they have been taught about God with what happened to them.

My recommendation is for them to tell God that they are angry with him. He can handle it. He knows that they are having these thoughts and struggles. He even invites us to come to him with such concerns. In Matthew 11:28, he says for us to come to him when we are under such heavy burdens. He wants to ease the weight.

The backdrop that I "paint" for those who are struggling with the God-issue because of anger, is to realize it is the same God who stood by and allowed his Son to go to the cross. It is the same God who could have delivered Jesus from the hands of those who were beating him into a pulp, spitting in his face, tearing his clothes off him, and forcefully placing a crown of thorns unto his head. He is the same God with whom they are having a problem.

I also remind them that we live in a fallen (sinful) world inhabited by very wicked people who have a free will to carry out their wickedness. It is also true that there is a Devil who incites, encourages and applauds this kind of wickedness.

The good news is that one day God will put an end to this and will hold everyone accountable for his or her behavior. He will be the final judge. No one will get away with the evil they do. Here is the best part of the news. If we put our trust in Jesus Christ and accept him as our Savior and Lord, we will be forgiven for all our sins, not have to face such judgment and will forever live with him in a place where there will be no more pain.

As part of my continuing education, I participated in the PAIRS® Foundation intensive training program. This training was centered on relationship enhancement.

One of the segments focused on what is termed "Emotional Allergy" (EA). I am not sure if this is unique to the foundation, but I thought that it summed up what most people who have experienced trauma go through. I know it has for me.

I have spoken to many people who have shared what would be described as an EA when they encountered their perpetrator or saw, heard, or smelled something that reminded them of their traumatic experience. These reminders are called "Triggers" because it sets off certain reactions within the body.

The body is made to protect itself from harm as much as it possibly can. Whenever it experiences a "Trigger", the automatic nervous system sends impulses throughout the body, which prepares it to fight or flee. This is referred to as the "fight or flight" syndrome. I would add a third component – freeze. Sometimes that is what the body does. It freezes up.

The body will tense itself because of the anxious feelings that arise whenever these triggers are activated. This would be referred to as an EA.

An example of this would be a child who grew up with an alcoholic parent and was abused whenever that parent became intoxicated. This child could have an EA whenever they are in the presence of someone that is intoxicated. This is especially more intense if they are in a relationship with someone who abuses alcohol.

As an adult he or she may react in ways that others may not understand because they are having an EA reaction.

Words takes on a whole new meaning for sexual trauma victims. When they hear phrases such as "this is a safe place", "Daddy or your teacher (or anyone in authority) loves you", "You can sleep in my bed or with me", etc., they are not hearing what is intended (assuming it is now coming from an innocent person). They can react in ways that may surprise the one making those statements. They are having an EA reaction.

This is similar to someone who has an allergy to pollen or dust. That person begins to sneeze almost uncontrollably while others around them do not. As an observer, you may begin to wonder what led to such a reaction. Why is this only happening to that one person? The answer lies in the fact that they are the ones with the allergy.

This is also true of EA.

From the above example, only the person with the allergy knows what is happening until they inform others. At times, a victim who is having these allergic reactions, may become hostile, angry, or simply treat others in a manner that is uncalled for. This would be called deflection. It is a means of diverting attention from the real problem (issue) to something or someone else.

One of reasons why the emotions of anger and fear persists is that the victim is looking for justice. They want to see the perpetrator pay for what they had done to them.

These heightened emotions can be reduced if they have a sense of justice or if the perpetrator shows genuine remorse, apologizes, and request forgiveness.

Another way of reducing these emotions is by neutralizing them with the virtues of empathy, sympathy, and compassion. This is very difficult to do but it is possible through forgiveness as will be discussed in chapter eleven.

As a therapist, I would strongly suggest the help of a trained professional who could help normalize some of these feelings.

I know that someone reading this, may have a difficult time embracing seeing a counselor / therapist. I know that I did at one time.

Growing up in Jamaica, going to see a therapist, psychologist, or a psychiatrist, had a negative connotation. This usually means that you were mentally sick; at least this is what we were told. One of the common sayings was, "only crazy people go to see these professionals".

How unfortunate this is. With this mindset, so many people continue to suffer in silence when they do not have to.

If this happens to be you, please get some help today. Think about it this way. When you are physically sick, you go to see a physician. When you have a toothache, you go to see a dentist. These people take care of physical issues. When you have a spiritual question or issue, you would go to a spiritual leader. The question is, "who do you go to see when you are in emotional pain?"

Your professional therapist / counselor have been trained to take care of these issues. Remember, you are mind, body and spirit. You are a triune being.

One of my favorite sayings that I use over and over again whenever I teach on Anger Management or simply talk about anger, is this: "He who angers you to react negatively, conquers you". This is one emotion we must rule over and not allow it to rule over us.

CHAPTER ELEVEN

Murder He Wrote

23 *Two years later, when Absalom's sheep were being sheared at Baal-hazor near Ephraim, Absalom invited all the king's sons to come to a feast.* **24** *He went to the king and said, "My sheep-shearers are now at work. Would the king and his servants please come to celebrate the occasion with me?"*

25 *The king replied, "No, my son. If we all came, we would be too much of a burden on you." Absalom pressed him, but the king wouldn't come, though he sent his thanks*

26 *"Well, then," Absalom said, "if you can't come, how about sending my brother Amnon instead?" "Why Amnon?" the king asked.* **27** *But Absalom kept on pressing the king* until he finally agreed to let all his sons attend, including Amnon.

28 Absalom told his men, "Wait until Amnon gets drunk; then at my signal, kill him! Don't be afraid. I'm the one who has given the command. Take courage and do it!" 29 So at Absalom's signal they murdered Amnon. Then the other sons of the king jumped on their mules and fled.

Absalom developed an incredible hatred for Amnon for disgracing Tamar, but he did not say anything to him. Amnon was unaware of how much Absalom knew. Absalom chose to keep it that way.

He had been thinking about what Amnon had done to his sister. These thoughts never left him. Every time he looked either at Amnon or his sister Tamar, he would have flashbacks of the look on Tamar's face: the look of fear, disbelief, numbness, and pain.

He, Absalom, replayed the scenario over and over again in his mind. He could hear Tamar sobbing on his chest, while feeling the tears drenching his shirt. He could remember how tightly he tried to hold her without hurting her, trying to calm her down, while reassuring her that he would be there for her. He remembered his conversation with Tamar.

"What's wrong little sis? What's the matter? Why are you mourning? Don't tell me Amnon forced himself on you. I know dad had sent you to see him"

"For now baby, don't say anything to anyone. Keep this to yourself. He is your half-brother. Don't let this upset you so much! C'mon let's go home"

This flashback only intensified his feelings of hatred for his half-brother Amnon. He nursed this hatred for two years.

Be careful with whom you hang out or with whom you associate. Not every invitation given to you must be accepted

The longer you keep hatred in your heart, the more you give the Devil room to plant seeds of evil in it.

Hatred is a primary emotion, which leads to the secondary emotion we know as anger. Paul warns us about this in the book of Ephesians 4:26 *"Go ahead and be angry. You do well to be angry--but don't use your anger as fuel for revenge. And don't stay angry. Don't go to bed angry. 27 Don't give the Devil that kind of foothold in your life."*

He will plant suggestions in your mind as to how you can deal with your hatred – what you can and should do about it. The Devil never suggests anything that is good or anything that honors God. He is incapable of such. What he will offer us and should we give in, may make us feel better temporarily, but it only hurts us in the long run.

Unfortunately for more than two years Absalom went to bed angry. While lying on his bed he planned how he would get even with Amnon. He plotted and schemed for the right time and moment.

He came up with the idea of a party and sent out invitations to his family and friends. His intention was to get Amnon drunk and then when the appropriate time came, he would give the signal to his "boys" to move in for the kill. David was also invited to the party.

The time came.

Amnon and other family members showed up. There were an abundance of food and alcoholic drinks. Absalom made sure that Amnon had much to drink. He may have suggested a drinking contest between Amnon and one of his men. He wanted him drunk.

How many stories have you heard of people especially women, who were encouraged to drink more than they should, only to find themselves being taken advantage of and for some, have led to their death? This also could happen by having your drink "spiked" with a drug commonly known as the "date rape drug," – rohypnol, which leads to a loss of consciousness.

As the party progressed, Absalom gave his "boys" the signal. Without hesitation, they began an argument with Amnon who, being so drunk, got into it with them. He challenged them to a fight using very colorful words to describe what he thought of them. As the fight ensued, Amnon was stabbed to death.

The other family members, who were not aware of all that had happened or why this was occurring, fled the scene before they too were killed. That is what they thought would happen to them if they stayed.

Here is a warning – be careful with whom and from whom you accept invitations. Not every invitation given to you must be accepted. You don't know what is planned for you.

Also remember what you sow, you also will reap and most of the time it is more than you sow that you reap. What goes around comes around.

Amnon invited Tamar to his house with the intention of raping her, which he did. Absalom invited Amnon to his house with the intention of killing him, which he did. The table was now turned. Absalom failed to realize that evil is not overcome with evil, but with good.

Here is what the Bible has to say on the matter. This is just one of the many references:

*"**Never pay back evil for evil to anyone**. Do things in such a way that everyone can see you are honorable. Do your part to live in peace with everyone, as much as possible. Dear friends, never avenge yourselves. Leave that to God. For it is written, "I will take vengeance; I will repay those who deserve it," says the Lord. Instead do what the Scriptures say: "If your enemies are hungry, feed them. If they are thirsty, give them something to drink, and they will be ashamed of what they have done to you."* **(Romans 12:17-21)**

Don't let evil get the best of you, but conquer evil by doing good.

CHAPTER TWELVE

For"GIFT"ness

> *Forgiveness is an act of the will, & the will can function regardless of the temperature of the heart.*
>
> *- Corrie Ten Boom*

Forgiveness is not a feeling. It is a choice. It is a decision of the will. Tamar had to choose to forgive.

Forgiveness is not forgetting the offense; forgiveness is deciding to not use the offense in destructive ways – for manipulation; to hold over ones head. This will be a decision that has to be re-affirmed over and over again because of the strong pull to revisit the issue.

So many people think that because they have the memory of the incident, they must not have forgiven. This is simply not true. You may have those reoccurring thoughts for quite some time. This does not mean you haven't forgiven. It means that you have to remind yourself that you have forgiven that person, and that you can begin to behave accordingly. Forgiveness is not "Forgetness" (I made up that word). The mind records and stores information, which is quite difficult to erase.

Do you think Tamar would ever forget what Amnon did to her? I hardly think so. However, she will have to repeatedly remind herself of her decision to forgive him.

One gentleman said to me after hearing me talk about the issue of forgiveness, that he told some one who had offended him that he *"would never forget that he had forgiven him"*.

When you forgive someone, you have come to the place where you have settled the matter in your mind and know that the offender can never pay the debt they owe you. "Something" was taken from you that cannot be replaced or returned.

No matter how hard Amnon may try, he could never pay the debt he owed Tamar. Nothing he did would be satisfactory. He would come up short. So it is with anyone who has offended you; they can never pay the debt they owe you.

Tamar, like anyone else, would have to settle the matter in her heart; she will have to choose to release Amnon, of this debt, and not hold it against him anymore. It is never easy. That is why forgiveness has to be a choice; a decision of the will. It is a gift to the offender. Does he/she deserve it? No! That is why it is a gift. Because it is a gift that is given, I have coined the word forGIFTness to explain forgiveness.

ForGIFTness is a forward motion. It is the vehicle that moves or propels you forward. It moves you from the place of "stuckness" to "unstuckness".

Having received forgiveness yourself (assuming you have), you want the offender to also feel what you have felt. For that to happen, you have to offer it as a gift. The question that you have to wrestle with is this, "would you like to give that gift to the person who had hurt you so that they too can feel the effects of forgiveness?" You can make that happen.

More importantly, forgiveness is granted and becomes more palatable when it is put within the context of the suffering Jesus endured on the cross. No one will ever experience what he went through. It was more than the physical pain. Many people throughout history have gone through the physical pain of crucifixion, but none have volunteered to do such for someone else, like Jesus did.

The difference is, no one was like Jesus. He never sinned. He never did anything wrong. He did nothing whatsoever to deserve what he went through. He was perfect. He took our place. We should have been on the cross paying for violating God's laws. The cross he took upon himself was punishment for our sins.

> *Forgiveness is also two-dimensional. It is first decisional and secondly, emotional.*

While he hung on the cross, in excruciating pain and utter embarrassment, he uttered these words, "Father, forgive them, for they do not know what they are doing!" (Luke 23:34) Jesus forgave those who had done such wrong to him.

One of the "come-backs" I hear so often is that "I'm not Jesus." I agree. You are not; neither am I. However, he makes this statement, "no servant is greater than his master," (John 15:20a) meaning, if he - the Master, went through such, why do we think we will be exempt. Even though we are not Jesus or come even close, we are instructed to strive to be like him.

Forgiveness is more for the "forgiver" than it is for the "forgivee." The one, who needs to forgive, carries the weight of the offense everyday of their lives. He or she is affected and impacted by what was done to them. They cannot get past it. Sometimes, they are unable to function. This weight can become very tiresome. It is a burden.

Forgiveness is also two-dimensional. It is first decisional and secondly, emotional. The former is commanded by scripture that we do. We *must* forgive. The latter is what we will have to work through, frequently reminding ourselves of the decision made to forgive.

This emotional reoccurrence is sometimes misconstrued for un-forgiveness. When we are reminded emotionally of the offense, we think this confirms un-forgiveness. However, this is farthest from the truth. This will take time. It cannot be rushed. As we behave in a forgiving manner, the emotions surrounding un-forgiveness will decrease in strength.

The depth of the pain that resulted in the need to offer forgiveness requires a deeper commitment to forgive. The strength of the emotions surrounding forgiveness has to be neutralized by the virtues of empathy (putting yourself in the other person's shoes), sympathy (feeling sorry for), and compassion (doing something for). You can read more about this topic at the **blog site http://www.regainhope.com**

Flooding the mind with alternative thoughts about the offender is another way of moving forward with for"gift"ness. This is done by thinking of the person or persons as being somewhat dysfunctional in their thinking to have done what they did. One person puts it this way: "they are sick; no one in their right mind could ever do such a thing". When they began to "flood" their mind with such thoughts, it helped decrease the power of the emotions currently being experienced.

And Finally, Why We Forgive

Jesus told a story found in Matthew 18, to illustrate forgiveness. In this story, he shared about a king who was owed many thousands of dollars. The king called the person who owed him the money to settle his account or face long-term prison sentence. Not only would he have to go to jail, but his family would have to as well.

The man who owed the king pleaded his case on the merits that he did not have the money to pay his debts.

The king had mercy (pity) on him, and forgave the debt. He realized the man could not pay the debt so he released him from it. He - the king - made that decision. The man thanked the king and, with a deep sigh of relief, left the courtyard.

On his way home, he ran into a friend of his who owed him about a hundred dollars. He asked the man for his money. The man who owed him pleaded with him to forgive the debt because he did not have the money to pay him.

On hearing this, he – the forgiven man - became enraged. He had the man arrested and thrown in prison.

Someone who witnessed what happened and knew what the king had done, reported it to the king. The king sent for the man he had forgiven the enormous debt. He - the king - was furious. He could not believe what had happened. He wanted to verify the report for himself.

He queried the man, and found out that this was indeed true. He was hoping it was not. The confirmation only enraged him more.

He commanded that the man and his family be taken and placed in jail until he paid every last cent. This meant he would die in jail, because he did not have the money.

Jesus then said, "this is what will happen to us, when we fail to forgive others from our hearts" – Matthew 18:35. We will not necessarily go to jail, but we will feel like we *are* in jail - imprisoned to our thoughts, until we release the offender from our heart. This is a torturing experience.

It is torturing to us when we fail to forgive, because God deems it so. When he compares what He did for us by sending Jesus to die for our debts - the billion dollars kind of debt, to how we fail to forgive someone from a hundred dollar kind of debt, it leaves Him no option but to "sentence" us.

This is one of the dilemmas that Tamar faced. Maybe you are facing a similar dilemma. Choose to forgive. You are the beneficiary of such.

Only the forgiven can truly forgive. Forgive, because you have been forgiven. Forgiveness is a choice!

My Story on Forgiveness

I remember that as a teen I was taught by my parents not to hate. This lesson happens to be one that I will never forget. It was not just being told, "you should not hate!" but it was one that was modeled for me.

There is a saying that goes like this, "children learn more about life by what you do, than what you say" or "a lesson is more caught than taught." I learned about not hating by what I saw from my parents in the following story.

My dad operated his own transportation business. He was the owner and operator. He would transport passengers from one location to the next, making regular stops on the way.

He would leave home before daybreak, almost every day except Sundays and sometimes-another day within the week. He would return from a long day of work at nightfall. He was a very hardworking man. In looking back, I realize the sacrifices he made to take care of his family.

This was his livelihood. If he did not work these long hours, my mom's salary as a schoolteacher would not be adequate to take care of all the financial obligations that they had.

One day while my dad was on his way to Kingston - the capital city of Jamaica, he was ambushed by three or four men, and severely beaten.

These men had been traveling the opposite direction when someone who was driving a passenger van like my dad's, almost forced them off the road. The roads in Jamaica are winding, narrow, and can be dangerous. It requires great skills at certain points to negotiate traffic.

They were angry because of this and began giving chase. My dad had no idea what was happening so he drove at the speed at which he normally does. It was almost daybreak.

It took a while for these men to catch up with my dad because they had to wait until it was safe to turn around.

Once they saw what looked like the vehicle that had almost ran them off the road, they overtook it and blocked the road, which forced my dad to stop. He could not get around them.

They jumped out of their vehicle, raced to my dad's door, and dragged him out. Once he was out, they began to kick, pummel, and beat him in his head with a brick. This all happened so fast, the passengers on the mini-bus, did not have time enough to respond. They were in a state of shock or just did not want to get involved.

They left my dad on the road beside his vehicle, bleeding profusely. He was eventually taken to the hospital where he was admitted. He received several stitches and had to remain hospitalized to recuperate.

The men were finally caught and arrested. They were charged and sentenced to jail. I do not remember all the specifics as to the sentencing. This I *do* remember. I was angry, very angry. I am not sure what I would have done if I could get to these men even though I was not as big as they were. I had hatred in my heart for them. I plotted in my mind, what I would one day do if I could get to them.

After some time had passed, my dad and mom realized that we were struggling with unforgiveness and hatred towards these men. They gathered us all together, and told us that we should not hate. When I heard my dad, who had been the innocent victim say that, I was dumbfounded.

"How do you not hate them," I protested. "Look what they did to you. Do you remember that day?"

My dad and mom reminded us of what the Bible taught about forgiveness and what God expected of us. This took me off-guard. It took me some time to process, but eventually I realize that we have been called to forgive.

They reminded us that Jesus forgave those who had beaten him and then crucified him.

I have never forgotten this and when I feel like not forgiving those who hurt me, I remember this story and more importantly, what Jesus did.

Jesus made this statement in Matthew 11:28, *"Come to me, all of you who are weary and carry heavy burdens, and I will give you rest."* Jesus wants to give everyone rest from the task of carrying such burdens, but it can only be done by accepting his invitation.

We forgive because we have been forgiven.

CHAPTER THIRTEEN

Conclusion

Rape is never justified. No matter the circumstances that may have led up to the incident, no one should ever be subjected to such violation. It is even more devastating when it is at the hand of a family member or acquaintance. These are people that you trust and with whom you should feel safe. Unfortunately, this was not the case of Tamar as you just read.

Talking about issues like this, is never easy. There are so many emotional, mental, and physiological aspects to rape. It could be a very exhaustive work to try and cover all aspects of it. However the key is that we recognize the traumatic impact rape can have on a person. It can have long-lasting impact and manifest itself emotionally, relationally, mentally, physically, spiritually or any of the above combination.

Unless the context is provided, one could be diagnosed or treated for symptoms while missing the root cause – trauma. If this happens, it could be more harmful than helpful.

I cannot over-emphasize the importance of finding competent healthcare workers who will look at the broader aspect of what maybe going on with clients and not just settle for a single explanation. This will require more than one session. It could take several months or years to work through this very difficult phase. Even then there are no guarantees.

Here is where my bias for a Christian Therapist comes in. The pain and deep hurt of trauma such as rape need supernatural intervention. As good a therapist as one can be, he or she is unable to reach the place of hurt that only God can. A Christian Therapist combines his or her skills along with the power of prayer and the use of God's word to provide comfort and healing like nothing else can. True freedom can only be experienced through opening one-self to the power of the Holy Spirit.

In addition to the above, therapy will be more effective, if clients accomplishes assigned tasks in between sessions. Most therapists will give clients "homework" to assist in a change of behavior and thinking. This will help reinforce what was talked about within the session and it is where most of the success will occur. Be patient with the process.

As mentioned before, if you are struggling with similar issues, please get help immediately. If it is someone you know, please encourage him or her to get help as well.

A great way to help in the reduction of painful experiences is to read the Psalms and make prayer a regular part of your daily routine. Pray short prayers throughout the day rather than set times. Make it spontaneous and conversational, talking to God as you would a friend. You can talk as you walk, drive, exercise and even work. This will be a great therapeutic tool.

In addition you may want to re-read chapters nine, ten, and twelve especially chapter twelve on forGIFTness.

You may have heard the saying that "time heals all wounds". I do know what most people who say this are trying to do. They are in their best effort trying to offer some words of comfort. I'm not sure people who are going through a painful situation receive this well. Therefore, I want to offer another way of saying it that may be more comforting. "HEALING TAKES TIME!"

Be patient with the process while remembering that God is our Refuge and Strength, a very present help in the time of difficulties, troubles, pain, etc. (Psalm 46:1-3)

Let him comfort you today!

APPENDIX

Tamar and Amnon's Story

2 Samuel 13:1 – 29 (New Living Translation)

¹ *Now David's son Absalom had a beautiful sister named Tamar. And Amnon, her half brother, fell desperately in love with her.* ² *Amnon became so obsessed with Tamar that he became ill. She was a virgin, and Amnon thought he could never have her.*

³ *But Amnon had a very crafty friend—his cousin Jonadab. He was the son of David's brother Shimea.*[a] ⁴ *One day Jonadab said to Amnon, "What's the trouble? Why should the son of a king look so dejected morning after morning?"*

So Amnon told him, "I am in love with Tamar, my brother Absalom's sister."

⁵ *"Well," Jonadab said, "I'll tell you what to do. Go back to bed and pretend you are ill. When your father comes to see you, ask him to let Tamar come and prepare some food for you. Tell him you'll feel better if she prepares it as you watch and feeds you with her own hands."*

⁶ *So Amnon lay down and pretended to be sick. And when the king came to see him, Amnon asked him, "Please let my sister Tamar come and cook my favorite dish[b] as I watch. Then I can eat it from her own hands."* ⁷ *So David agreed and sent Tamar to Amnon's house to prepare some food for him.*

⁸ *When Tamar arrived at Amnon's house, she went to the place where he was lying down so he could watch her mix some dough. Then she baked his favorite dish for him.* ⁹ *But when she set the serving tray before him, he refused to eat. "Everyone get out of here," Amnon told his servants. So they all left.*

¹⁰ *Then he said to Tamar, "Now bring the food into my bedroom and feed it to me here." So Tamar took his favorite dish to him.* ¹¹ *But as she was feeding him, he grabbed her and demanded, "Come to bed with me, my darling sister."*

¹² *"No, my brother!" she cried. "Don't be foolish! Don't do this to me! Such wicked things aren't done in Israel.* ¹³ *Where could I go in my shame? And you would be called one*

of the greatest fools in Israel. Please, just speak to the king about it, and he will let you marry me."

¹⁴ But Amnon wouldn't listen to her, and since he was stronger than she was, he raped her. ¹⁵ Then suddenly Amnon's love turned to hate, and he hated her even more than he had loved her. "Get out of here!" he snarled at her.

¹⁶ "No, no!" Tamar cried. "Sending me away now is worse than what you've already done to me."

But Amnon wouldn't listen to her. ¹⁷ He shouted for his servant and demanded, "Throw this woman out, and lock the door behind her!"

¹⁸ So the servant put her out and locked the door behind her. She was wearing a long, beautiful robe,[] as was the custom in those days for the king's virgin daughters. ¹⁹ But now Tamar tore her robe and put ashes on her head. And then, with her face in her hands, she went away crying.

²⁰ Her brother Absalom saw her and asked, "Is it true that Amnon has been with you? Well, my sister, keep quiet for now, since he's your brother. Don't you worry about it." So Tamar lived as a desolate woman in her brother Absalom's house.

²¹ When King David heard what had happened, he was very angry.[d] ²² And though Absalom never spoke to Amnon about this, he hated Amnon deeply because of what he had done to his sister.

Absalom's Revenge on Amnon

²³ Two years later, when Absalom's sheep were being sheared at Baal-hazor near Ephraim, Absalom invited all the king's sons to come to a feast. ²⁴ He went to the king and said, "My sheep-shearers are now at work. Would the king and his servants please come to celebrate the occasion with me?"

²⁵ The king replied, "No, my son. If we all came, we would be too much of a burden on you." Absalom pressed him, but the king would not come, though he gave Absalom his blessing.

²⁶ "Well, then," Absalom said, "if you can't come, how about sending my brother Amnon with us?"

"Why Amnon?" the king asked. ²⁷ But Absalom kept on pressing the king until he finally agreed to let all his sons attend, including Amnon. So Absalom prepared a feast fit for a king.[e]

²⁸ Absalom told his men, "Wait until Amnon gets drunk; then at my signal, kill him! Don't be afraid. I'm the one who

has given the command. Take courage and do it!" ²⁹ *So at Absalom's signal they murdered Amnon. Then the other sons of the king jumped on their mules and fled.*

ABOUT THE AUTHOR

Kingsley Grant is CEO / President of Helping Families Improve and a Licensed Marriage and Family Therapist, Author, Motivational Speaker, Certified Motivational Life Coach with the American Association of Christian Counselor, Workshop Presenter, and Clergy Member. He is also a Certified PAIRS Foundation Best Practice Facilitator.

He is from Jamaica West Indies, and has lived in the United States for more than half of his life.

He is the Author of the "**10 Day Devotional**" designed for teens and young adults while on Retreats or Short-Term Mission Trips.

He is available to speak to agencies, churches, business, schools and any other organization that could benefit from motivational speaking on the topic of hope.

Kingsley's strategy is to outline the process of moving from a place of hopelessness (less hope) to one of hopefulness (full hope). This he does by helping individuals **Modify** their thought process, **Adjust** their attitudes, and **Position** themselves. He calls this "The M.A.P Process".

He believes that people map their way each day without thinking about it as they have formed habits around new behaviors. An example of this would be driving to work and encountering an accident on the main road. Immediately mapping begins to take place. We start to think of another way to our destination. Upon such discovery, we seek to implement that alternative path as soon as possible.

What if a person could begin to do this in their life — at work, school, or any other place that they find themselves? They would never be the same again. That is his mission — to give people who are "stuck" a chance to become "unstuck".

Contact Information

Website:

www.helpingothershope.com

www.regainhope.com

EMAIL:

info@helpingothershope.com

9/25/11

Made in the USA
Charleston, SC
08 September 2011